Illustrated Dictionary

Illustrated Dictionary

To help you with your writing you can either use the illustrated dictionary or flip the book over to look at the key word themes.

The illustrated dictionary is organised as follows:

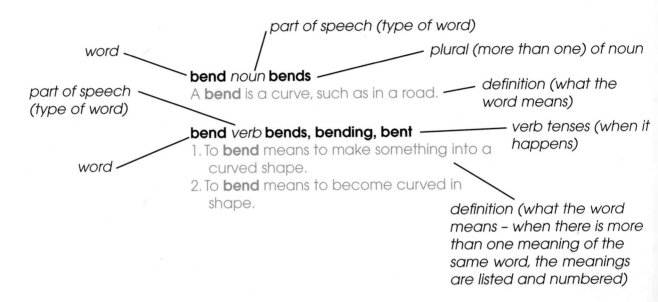

The parts of speech

Noun
This is a word used for naming a person, animal, place or thing (eg Wendy, dog, London, train).

Pronoun
This is a word used to describe a person or thing, without giving their name (eg I, she, them, it).

Adjective
This is a word used to describe a *noun* or *pronoun* (eg asleep, busy, cheerful). *The* **busy** *chef had a lot of meals to cook.*

Verb
This is a word used to describe action or existence. Sometimes it is called a 'doing' word (eg grow, kick, told, was).

Adverb
This is a word that usually tells you more about a *verb*. Sometimes it tells you about other words (but not a *noun* or a *pronoun*) (eg almost, daily, exactly, quickly). *She enjoyed her* **daily** *run around the park.*

Preposition
This is a word that shows what one person or thing has to do with another (eg above, over, through).

Conjunction
This is a word used to join words and parts of a sentence (eg because, when, where).

On each page you will find a 'dictionary fun' activity to help you practise your dictionary skills.

Aa

ability *noun* **abilities**
An **ability** is a skill or talent someone has for doing something.

able *adjective*
Someone who has a skill or is clever is **able**.

aboard *adverb and preposition*
Someone or something is **aboard** when on or in a ship, aircraft, train or other vehicle.

above *adverb and preposition*
The bird flies **above** the bush.

abroad *adverb*
Someone who has gone to a foreign country has gone **abroad**.

absent *adjective*
Someone who is not present is **absent**.

accident *noun* **accidents**
An **accident** is an event that is not expected to happen, especially when damage is done.

ache *noun* **aches**
An **ache** is a pain.

across *preposition*
She lives in a house **across** the road from me.

act *noun* **acts**
1. An **act** is something that is done.
2. An **act** is a law made by parliament.
3. An **act** is part of a play or show.

act *verb* **acts, acting, acted**
To **act** means to perform, usually in front of an audience.

active *adjective*
Something that is moving about is **active**.

actor *noun* **actors**
A person who acts on stage, in television or films is an **actor**.

address *noun* **addresses**
An **address** describes where a house or business is by naming its street, town, and postal code.

address *verb* **addresses, addressing, addressed**
1. To **address** an envelope means to write the address on it.
2. To **address** someone means to speak to that person.

adjective *noun* **adjectives**
An **adjective** is a word which describes a noun.

admire *verb* **admires, admiring, admired**
To **admire** someone or something means to think very highly of a person or object.

adult *noun* **adults**
An **adult** is a person or animal who is fully grown.

adventure *noun* **adventures**
An **adventure** is an exciting or dangerous event.

adverb *noun* **adverbs**
An **adverb** is a word which is added to a verb or adjective to describe it in more detail.

advertisement *noun* **advertisements**
An **advertisement** is a public notice, often to encourage people to buy a certain object.

advice *noun* **advice**
Advice is information which recommends what someone should do.

aerial *noun* **aerials**
An **aerial** is the wire or rod which receives or transmits radio and television signals.

affection *noun* **affections**
An **affection** for something is a love or liking of it.

afford *verb* **affords, affording, afforded**
To **afford** something means to have enough money to be able to buy it.

Dictionary fun
What type of words are **white, heavy** and **more**?

?

a b c d e f g h i j k l m n o p q r s t u v w x y z

afraid *adjective*
Someone who is frightened is **afraid**.

after *adverb and preposition*
Something that is behind or later than, is **after**.

afternoon *noun* **afternoons**
An **afternoon** is the part of the day between noon and about 6 pm.

afterwards *adverb*
Something that happens at a later time happens **afterwards**.

again *adverb*
Something that happens more than once happens **again**.

age *noun* **ages**
The **age** of a person, animal or object is the length of its life.

agree *verb* **agrees, agreeing, agreed**
To **agree** with someone means to share the same idea or opinion.

ahead *adverb*
Something or someone who is further forward is **ahead**.

aim *verb* **aims, aiming, aimed**
To **aim** means to point towards a target.

air *noun*
Air is the mixture of gases around the earth.

aircraft *noun* **aircraft**
An **aircraft** is a machine which can fly in the air.

airline *noun* **airlines**
An **airline** is an organisation providing aircraft for people to use on one or more routes.

airport *noun* **airports**
An **airport** has buildings where people go to catch planes, and runways from which planes take off and land.

alarm *noun* **alarms**
An **alarm** is a warning sound or signal.

alarm *verb* **alarms, alarming, alarmed**
To **alarm** means to frighten.

album *noun* **albums**
An **album** is a blank book for sticking in things like photographs or stamps.

alive *adjective*
Something that is living is **alive**.

all *adjective*
All is every one of something. *All people breathe air.*

alligator *noun* **alligators**
An **alligator** is a reptile similar to a crocodile.

allow *verb* **allows, allowing, allowed**
To **allow** means to give permission.

almost *adverb*
When something has nearly happened, it has **almost** happened.

alone *adjective*
Someone is **alone** when nobody else is there.

along *adverb and preposition*
Something that goes from one point to another goes **along** it.

aloud *adverb*
When something is spoken so others can hear, it is said **aloud**.

alphabet *noun* **alphabets**
An **alphabet** is the letters of a language arranged in order.

Dictionary fun

Which words (on this page) have only one consonant?

? **?** ? ?

a b c d e f g h i j k l m n o p q r s t u v w x y z

already *adverb*
Something has happened **already** when it has happened before now.

although *conjunction*
Although means in spite of the fact.

always *adverb*
Something that happens at all times or again and again happens **always**.

ambulance *noun*
ambulances
An **ambulance** is a vehicle for carrying sick or injured people.

among *preposition*
1. Someone is **among** something when surrounded by it.
2. Things can be shared between or **among** people.

amount *noun* **amounts**
An **amount** is a quantity of a thing.

amount *verb* **amounts, amounting, amounted**
To **amount** is to add up to.

amuse *verb* **amuses, amusing, amused**
To amuse is to make someone laugh or smile.

ancient *adjective*
Something is **ancient** when it is very old.

anger *noun* **anger**
Anger is a strong feeling that makes people want to fight or shout.

angle *noun* **angles**
An **angle** is the space between two lines or surfaces that meet.

angry *adjective*
Someone who is very cross and annoyed is **angry**.

animal *noun*
animals
An **animal** is a living creature that can breathe and move.

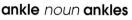

ankle *noun* **ankles**
An **ankle** is the joint connecting the leg and the foot.

announce *verb* **announces, announcing, announced**
To **announce** is to make something known to several people.

annoy *verb* **annoys, annoying, annoyed**
To **annoy** is to bother or irritate someone.

another *adjective and pronoun*
One more of something, or a different one, is **another** of that thing.

answer *noun* **answers**
1. An **answer** is a reply to a question.
2. An **answer** is a solution to a problem.

answer *verb* **answers, answering, answered**
1. To **answer** is to reply to something.
2. To **answer** is to solve a problem.

ant *noun* **ants**
An **ant** is a small insect.

antelope *noun* **antelopes**
An **antelope** is a wild animal like a deer.

anxious *adjective*
Someone who is worried is **anxious**.

anybody/anyone *noun* and *pronoun*
Anybody is any person.

anything *pronoun*
Anything is a thing of any kind.

anywhere *adverb*
Someone who goes to any place goes **anywhere**.

ape *noun* **apes**
An **ape** is a monkey with long arms and no tail, such as a chimpanzee.

Dictionary fun
Which word has a silent **w**?

? ? ? ?

appear *verb* **appears, appearing, appeared**
1. To **appear** means to come into sight.
2. To **appear** means to be seen in a public place, such as on a stage or in a law court.
3. To **appear** means to seem.

appearance *noun* **appearances**
1. An **appearance** is when something comes into sight.
2. An **appearance** is the way someone looks or seems.

appetite *noun* **appetites**
An **appetite** is a longing for something, especially food.

apple *noun* **apples**
An **apple** is a firm, round fruit.

apricot *noun* **apricots**
An **apricot** is a soft orange-yellow fruit with a large stone in it.

apron *noun* **aprons**
An **apron** is a garment worn over the front of a person's clothes to keep them clean.

aquarium *noun* **aquariums** or **aquaria**
1. An **aquarium** is a glass tank for keeping fish in.
2. An **aquarium** is a building containing tanks of fish.

arch *noun* **arches**
An **arch** is the curved shape seen in bridges and buildings.

arch *verb* **arches, arching, arched**
To **arch** means to make a curved shape like an arch.

area *noun* **areas**
1. An **area** is a region of land.
2. An **area** is a measurement of the amount of space, usually in a flat shape.

argue *verb* **argues, arguing, argued**
To **argue** means to quarrel with someone.

arithmetic *noun*
Arithmetic is the study or use of numbers.

arm *noun* **arms**
1. An **arm** is the part of the body from the shoulder to the hand.

2. An **arm** is a weapon.

arm *verb* **arms, arming, armed**
To **arm** is to supply someone with weapons for fighting.

armchair *noun* **armchairs**
An **armchair** is a chair with supports for the arms.

army *noun* **armies**
An **army** is a large group of people, usually soldiers, trained to fight on land.

around *adverb and preposition*
Something that is on every side is **around**. *As I looked around the room, I could see all the pictures on the walls.*

arrange *verb* **arranges, arranging, arranged**
1. To **arrange** things means to put them in their proper place or order.
2. To **arrange** something means to make plans for it.

arrive *verb* **arrives, arriving, arrived**
To **arrive** means to come to the end of a journey.

arrow *noun* **arrows**
1. An **arrow** is a pointed stick that is shot from a bow.

2. An **arrow** is a sign in the shape of an arrow.

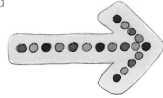

art *noun* **arts**
1. **Art** is a painting, drawing or model created by someone.
2. An **art** is a skill.

artist *noun* **artists**
An **artist** is a person who paints pictures.

Dictionary fun

How many words (on this page) start and finish with a vowel?

? ? ? ?

ask *verb* **asks, asking, asked**
To **ask** means to speak in order to find out or request something.

asleep *adjective*
Someone who is sleeping is **asleep**.

assembly *noun* **assemblies**
An **assembly** is a large gathering of people, especially school children at the beginning of the day.

astonish *verb* **astonishes, astonishing, astonished**
To **astonish** means to surprise or amaze.

astronaut *noun* **astronauts**
An **astronaut** is a person who travels in space.

ate *verb*
This is the past tense of the verb 'to eat' (see **eat**).

atlas *noun* **atlases**
An **atlas** is a book of maps.

atmosphere *noun* **atmospheres**
1. **Atmosphere** is the air around the earth that we breathe.
2. An **atmosphere** is the feeling a place has.

attack *noun* **attacks**
1. An **attack** is a sudden attempt to hurt or overpower someone.
2. An **attack** is a sudden illness or pain.

attack *verb* **attacks, attacking, attacked**
To **attack** means to start fighting in order to hurt or beat someone.

attention *noun* **attention**
Attention is the careful thought given to something or listening to someone.

attic *noun* **attics**
An **attic** is a room in the roof of a house.

attract *verb* **attracts, attracting, attracted**
1. To **attract** means to get someone's interest.
2. To **attract** means to pull something nearer.

attractive *adjective*
Something or someone that is very pleasing to look at is **attractive**.

audience *noun* **audiences**

An **audience** is the group of people who have come to look at or hear something, such as a concert.

aunt *noun* **aunts**
An **aunt** is the sister of your mother or father or the wife of your uncle.

author *noun* **authors**
An **author** is a person who writes stories or books.

avalanche *noun* **avalanches**
An **avalanche** is a sudden fall of snow down a mountain.

avenue *noun* **avenues**
An **avenue** is a road or driveway, usually with trees along each side of it.

average *adjective*
Something that is usual or ordinary is **average**.

awake *adjective*
Someone who is not asleep is **awake**.

away *adverb*
Someone who is at a distance or not at home is **away**.

awful *adjective*
Something that is very bad or dreadful is **awful**.

awkward *adjective*
1. Someone who is clumsy is **awkward**.
2. Someone who is difficult to deal with is **awkward**.
3. Something that causes problems is **awkward**.

axe *noun* **axes**
An **axe** is a sharp tool used for chopping wood.

Dictionary fun

What might contain Ireland, Britain Canada and Australia?

? **?** ? ?

Bb

baby *noun* **babies**
A **baby** is a very young child.

back *noun* **backs**
1. A **back** is the part of the body between the shoulders and the bottom.
2. The opposite of the **back** is the front.

backwards *adverb*
The opposite of forwards is **backwards**.

bad *adjective*
Something that is not good is **bad**.

badge *noun* **badges**
A **badge** is something worn on clothes to show what group a person belongs to or what position a person holds.

bag *noun* **bags**
A **bag** is a container for carrying things in.

bait *noun* **bait**
Bait is the food put on a hook to catch fish or in a trap to catch animals.

bake *verb* **bakes, baking, baked**
To **bake** means to cook in the oven.

baker *noun* **bakers**
A **baker** is a person whose work is to make bread, cakes and pies.

balance *noun* **balances**
A **balance** is a pair of scales for weighing things.

balance *verb* **balances, balancing, balanced**
To **balance** means to make or keep something steady or still.

balcony *noun* **balconies**
1. A **balcony** is a platform with railings round it outside an upstairs window.
2. A **balcony** is the upstairs seating area in a theatre or cinema.

bald *adjective*
Someone who has no hair is **bald**.

ball *noun* **balls**
1. A **ball** is a round object used in games such as football or tennis.
2. A **ball** is a large formal party with dancing.

balloon *noun* **balloons**
1. A **balloon** is a small rubber container that can be filled with air and played with.
2. A **balloon** is a large container filled with hot air or gas that floats in the sky and sometimes carries passengers in a basket.

bamboo *noun*
A **bamboo** is a tall plant with hollow stems or canes.

banana *noun* **bananas**
A **banana** is a long, curved fruit with a thick, yellow skin.

band *noun* **bands**
1. A **band** is a strip of material shaped in a loop.
2. A **band** is a group of people who play musical instruments together.

bandage *noun* **bandages**
A **bandage** is a strip of material for wrapping round a wound.

bank *noun* **banks**
1. A **bank** is a place that looks after people's money.
2. A **bank** is a sloping piece of ground, often on the edge of a pond or river.

bar *noun* **bars**
1. A **bar** is a long piece of hard material such as metal or chocolate.
2. A **bar** is a place that serves drinks.

bare *adjective*
Someone who has no clothes on is **bare**.

bargain *noun* **bargains**
1. A **bargain** is an object that is much cheaper than it usually costs.
2. A **bargain** is a promise or an agreement.

bark *noun* **barks**
1. A **bark** is the sound a dog makes.
2. A **bark** is the outer covering on a tree trunk.

bark *verb* **barks, barking, barked**
To **bark** means to make the sound of a dog.

Dictionary fun
Which word sounds like **hair**?

? ? ? ?

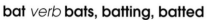

a b c d e f g h i j k l m n o p q r s t u v w x y z

barn *noun* **barns**
A **barn** is a large building on a farm for storing things and keeping animals in.

barrel *noun* **barrels**
1. A **barrel** is a large round container with flat ends.
2. A **barrel** is the narrow tube at the front of a gun.

base *noun* **bases**
A **base** is the lowest part of something.

basket *noun* **baskets**
A **basket** is a container often made of cane.

bat *noun* **bats**
1. A **bat** is an animal like a mouse with large wings.
2. A **bat** is a piece of wood used in games to hit a ball.

bat *verb* **bats, batting, batted**
To **bat** means to hit with a bat.

bath *noun* **baths**
A **bath** is a large container which is filled with water and used for sitting and washing in.

bath *verb* **baths, bathing, bathed**
To **bath** means to have or to give someone a bath.

bathroom *noun* **bathrooms**
A **bathroom** is the room where a person can have a bath or wash.

battery *noun* **batteries**
A **battery** is a container which stores electricity and is used to make things work.

beach *noun* **beaches**
A **beach** is the land on the edge of the sea usually covered in sand or pebbles.

bead *noun* **beads**
A **bead** is a round object with a hole through it, often threaded on a string to make a necklace.

beak *noun* **beaks**
A **beak** is the hard part of a bird's mouth.

bean *noun* **beans**
A **bean** is a vegetable that grows in long pods.

bear *noun* **bears**
A **bear** is a large, furry animal.

bear *verb* **bears, bearing, bore, born**
1. To **bear** means to give birth to.
2. To **bear** means to put up with.
3. To **bear** means to carry.

beard *noun* **beards**
A **beard** is the hair that grows on a man's face.

beat *verb* **beats, beating, beaten**
1. To **beat** means to hit someone or something several times.
2. To **beat** means to stir food quickly before cooking it.
3. To **beat** means to do better than someone.

beautiful *adjective*
Something that is very attractive or pleasant is **beautiful**.

because *conjunction*
Because means for the reason that. *I felt very full because I had eaten too much.*

bedroom *noun* **bedrooms**
A **bedroom** is a room for sleeping in.

bee *noun* **bees**
A **bee** is an insect that can fly and sting and that makes honey.

beef *noun* **beef**
Beef is the meat from a cow, bull or ox.

beehive *noun* **beehives**
A **beehive** is a box-shaped home for bees.

beetle *noun* **beetles**
A **beetle** is an insect with hard cases over its wings.

begin *verb* **begins, beginning, began, begun**
To **begin** means to start.

behave *verb* **behaves, behaving, behaved**
To **behave** means to act in a good or bad way.

Dictionary fun

Which words are compound words (can be split into smaller words)?

? **?** ? ?

a b c d e f g h i j k l m n o p q r s t u v w x y z

bell *noun* **bells**
A **bell** is a metal instrument that makes a ringing sound.

belong *verb* **belongs, belonging, belonged**
1. To **belong** to someone means to be owned by that person.
2. To **belong** to something means to be part of that group.
3. To **belong** means to be in the proper place.

belt *noun* **belts**
A **belt** is a band, often made of leather, worn round the waist.

bench *noun* **benches**
A **bench** is a long, hard seat for more than one person to sit on.

bend *noun* **bends**
A **bend** is a curve, such as in a road.

bend *verb* **bends, bending, bent**
1. To **bend** means to make something into a curved shape.
2. To **bend** means to become curved in shape.

berry *noun* **berries**
A **berry** is a small, round fruit with seeds in it.

beware *verb*
To **beware** of something means to be careful of it.

bicycle *noun* **bicycles**
A **bicycle** is a vehicle with two wheels which is ridden using pedals.

bird *noun* **birds**
A **bird** is an animal with wings and is covered with feathers.

birth *noun* **births**
A **birth** is when a baby leaves its mother's body and starts to breathe on its own.

birthday *noun* **birthdays**
A **birthday** is the date each year of a person's birth.

bite *verb* **bites, biting, bit, bitten**
1. To **bite** something means to cut into it with the teeth.
2. To **bite** means to sting.

blade *noun* **blades**
1. A **blade** is the flat, sharp part of a knife.
2. A **blade** is something that is shaped like a blade, such as a **blade** of grass.

blame *verb* **blames, blaming, blamed**
To **blame** means to say that something or someone made something bad happen.

blanket *noun* **blankets**
A **blanket** is a thick, warm cover used on a bed.

bleed *verb* **bleeds, bleeding, bled**
To **bleed** means to lose blood.

blind *noun* **blinds**
A **blind** is a screen that can be pulled or rolled down to cover a window.

blind *adjective*
A person who is unable to see is **blind**.

blindfold *verb* **blindfolds, blindfolding, blindfolded**
To **blindfold** means to cover someone's eyes so that the person cannot see.

blizzard *noun* **blizzards**
A **blizzard** is a very windy snowstorm.

block *noun* **blocks**
A **block** is a thick, solid lump of something, such as wood or stone.

block *verb* **blocks, blocking, blocked**
To **block** means to stop something getting through.

blood *noun* **blood**
Blood is the red liquid that flows round the body.

blot *noun* **blots**
A **blot** is a spot of ink that has been spilt.

blouse *noun* **blouses**
A **blouse** is a piece of clothing for the top half of the body worn by women and girls.

blow *verb* **blows, blowing, blew, blown**
1. To **blow** means to move in the wind.
2. To **blow** means to force air out of the mouth.

Dictionary fun

What type of animal are the duck and the goose?

? ? ? ?

blunt *adjective*
Something that is not sharp is **blunt**.

board *noun* **boards**
A **board** is a long, flat piece of wood or other material.

board *verb* **boards, boarding, boarded**
To **board** means to get on a bus, train, ship or plane.

boat *noun* **boats**
A **boat** is something made to float on water and can carry people or objects.

body *noun* **bodies**
A **body** is all of a person or animal, either alive or dead.

boil *noun* **boils**
A **boil** is a big spot on the skin.

boil *verb* **boils, boiling, boiled**
1. To **boil** means to heat a liquid until it bubbles and gives off steam.
2. To **boil** means to cook something in boiling water.

bone *noun* **bones**
A **bone** is one of the parts of a skeleton.

bonfire *noun* **bonfires**
A **bonfire** is a large fire in the open air.

book *noun* **books**
A **book** is a set of sheets of paper fixed together inside a cover.

book *verb* **books, booking, booked**
To **book** is to reserve a seat for a journey or in a theatre or cinema.

bookcase *noun* **bookcases**
A **bookcase** is a piece of furniture made to hold books.

bookshop *noun* **bookshops**
A **bookshop** is a shop in which books are sold.

boot *noun* **boots**
A **boot** is a kind of strong shoe, which also covers the ankle.

bore *verb*
This is the past tense of the verb 'to bear' (see **bear** (1)).

borrow *verb* **borrows, borrowing, borrowed**
To **borrow** is to use something that belongs to someone else and then give it back.

both *adjective and pronoun*
Both means the two, not just one.

bottle *noun* **bottles**
A **bottle** is a container for liquids which is usually narrower at the top.

bottom *noun* **bottoms**
1. A **bottom** is the part of the body that a person sits on.
2. The **bottom** is the lowest part of something.

bought *verb*
This is the past tense of the verb 'to buy' (see **buy**).

bounce *verb* **bounces, bouncing, bounced**
1. To **bounce** means to spring back after hitting a hard surface.
2. To **bounce** means to jump up and down.

bow *noun* **bows**
1. A **bow** is a bent piece of wood with a string joining the two ends, used for shooting arrows.
2. A **bow** is a wooden rod with hair tightly joining its ends, used to play stringed instruments.
3. A **bow** is a kind of knot with loops.

bow *verb* **bows, bowing, bowed**
To **bow** means to bend forwards politely when meeting someone.

bowl *noun* **bowls**
A **bowl** is a round, open container.

bowl *verb* **bowls, bowling, bowled**
To **bowl** means to throw the ball towards the batter, such as in cricket.

box *noun* **boxes**
A **box** is a container, usually with a lid.

box *verb* **boxes, boxing, boxed**
To **box** means to fight or punch with the fists.

boy *noun* **boys**
A **boy** is a male child.

Dictionary fun
In which word is there a silent **g**?

? ? ? ?

bracelet *noun* **bracelets**
A **bracelet** is a decorated band worn round the wrist or arm.

brain *noun* **brains**
A **brain** is the part of the body inside the head that controls all parts of the body.

brake *noun* **brakes**
A **brake** is the part of a vehicle that makes it slow down or stop.

branch *noun* **branches**
A **branch** is a part that sticks out from the main part, especially on a tree.

brass *noun* **brass**
Brass is a yellow metal.

brave *adjective*
Someone who can face danger or pain is **brave**.

bread *noun* **bread**
Bread is a food made by baking flour, yeast and water.

break *noun* **breaks**
A **break** is a short rest from work.

break *verb* **breaks, breaking, broke, broken**
1. To **break** something means to crack or smash it.
2. To **break** something like a law or promise means to fail to keep it.

breakfast *noun* **breakfasts**
A **breakfast** is the first meal of the day.

breath *noun* **breaths**
A **breath** is the air that someone breathes in and out.

breathe *verb* **breathes, breathing, breathed**
To **breathe** means to take air into the lungs through the nose or mouth and then let it out.

breeze *noun* **breezes**
A **breeze** is a gentle wind.

brick *noun* **bricks**
1. A **brick** is a block of baked clay used to build walls.

2. A **brick** is a toy in the shape of a small brick.

bride *noun* **brides**
A **bride** is the woman on the day of her wedding.

bridegroom *noun* **bridegrooms**
A **bridegroom** is the man on the day of his wedding.

bridge *noun* **bridges**
A **bridge** is something built to make a crossing over a railway, river or road.

brief *adjective*
Something that is short is **brief**.

briefcase *noun* **briefcases**
A **briefcase** is a small case for carrying papers.

bright *adjective*
1. Something that is shining is **bright**.
2. Someone who is clever is **bright**.

brim *noun* **brims**
A **brim** is the edge of something such as a container or a hat.

bring *verb* **brings, bringing, brought**
To **bring** means to go to fetch something.

broad *adjective*
Something that is wide is **broad**.

broadcast *noun* **broadcasts**
A **broadcast** is a radio or television show.

brooch *noun* **brooches**
A **brooch** is a decorative piece of jewellery pinned to clothing.

brook *noun* **brooks**
A **brook** is a stream.

broom *noun* **brooms**
A **broom** is a sweeping brush with a long handle.

Dictionary fun
Which word may be sliced, brown or white?

? **?** ? ?

a b c d e f g h i j k l m n o p q r s t u v w x y z

brother *noun* **brothers**
A **brother** is a man or boy who has the same parents as another person.

brought *verb*
This is the past tense of the verb 'to bring' (see **bring**).

bruise *noun* **bruises**
A **bruise** is a coloured mark on the skin, caused by a hard knock.

brush *noun* **brushes**
A **brush** is a tool with bristles and a handle used for sweeping, painting or brushing hair.

bubble *noun* **bubbles**
A **bubble** is a small ball of liquid filled with air.

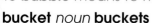

bubble *verb* **bubbles, bubbling, bubbled**
To **bubble** means to make bubbles.

bucket *noun* **buckets**
A **bucket** is a container with a handle for carrying liquid.

buckle *noun* **buckles**
A **buckle** is a fastener on a belt or strap.

bud *noun* **buds**
A **bud** is a flower or leaf before it has opened fully.

build *verb* **builds, building, built**
To **build** means to make something by putting parts together.

building *noun* **buildings**
A **building** is something that has been built, such as a house, factory or shop.

bull *noun* **bulls**
A **bull** is a male cow, ox, elephant or whale.

bullet *noun* **bullets**
A **bullet** is a small ball of metal which is shot from a gun.

bump *noun* **bumps**
A **bump** is a lump or swelling.

bump *verb* **bumps, bumping, bumped**
To **bump** means to knock into or against something by accident.

bunch *noun* **bunches**
A **bunch** is a group of things held together.

bundle *noun* **bundles**
A **bundle** is a group of things tied or wrapped together.

bungalow *noun* **bungalows**
A **bungalow** is a house with no upstairs.

burn *noun* **burns**
A **burn** is an injury caused by fire, heat or acid.

burn *verb* **burns, burning, burned** or **burnt**
1. To **burn** means to hurt or damage by fire or heat.
2. To **burn** means to be on fire.

burrow *noun* **burrows**
A **burrow** is a hole in the ground made by an animal to live in.

burst *verb* **bursts, bursting, burst**
To **burst** means to explode or break open.

bury *verb* **buries, burying, buried**
To **bury** means to put something in a hole in the ground and cover it over.

bus *noun* **buses**
A **bus** is a large road vehicle that people can pay to travel in.

bush *noun* **bushes**
A **bush** is a shrub or plant like a small tree.

business *noun* **businesses**
1. A **business** is someone's occupation.
2. A **business** is a shop, industry or firm.

busy *adjective*
Someone or something that has a lot to do or a lot going on is **busy**.

butcher *noun* **butchers**
A **butcher** is someone who sells meat.

butter *noun* **butter**
Butter is a food made from churned cream.

butterfly *noun* **butterflies**
A **butterfly** is an insect with large, coloured wings.

button *noun* **buttons**
A **button** is a small, round object sewn to clothes to fasten them.

buy *verb* **buys, buying, bought**
To **buy** something means to get it by giving money for it.

Dictionary fun

Which word describes a school, a theatre and a factory?

? ? ? ?

Cc

cabbage *noun* **cabbages**
A **cabbage** is a round vegetable with a lot of green or purple leaves.

cabin *noun* **cabins**
1. A **cabin** is a hut.
2. A **cabin** is a room in a ship or plane.

cactus *noun* **cacti**
A **cactus** is a prickly plant found in the desert.

café *noun* **cafés**
A **café** is a place that sells drinks, snacks and meals.

cage *noun* **cages**
A **cage** is a box with bars across it for keeping animals and birds in.

cake *noun* **cakes**
A **cake** is a mixture of flour, butter, eggs and sugar which is baked.

calculator *noun* **calculators**
A **calculator** is a small electronic machine that can help us with mathematics.

calf *noun* **calves**
1. A **calf** is a young cow, elephant, whale or seal.
2. A **calf** is the back part of the leg between the knee and the ankle.

call *verb* **calls, calling, called**
1. To **call** means to speak loudly.
2. To **call** means to speak to someone on the telephone.
3. To **call** means to give someone or something a name.

calm *adjective*
1. Something that is quiet or still is **calm**.
2. Something or someone who is not excited or panicky is **calm**.

camel *noun* **camels**
A **camel** is a large animal with one or two humps on its back.

camera *noun* **cameras**
A **camera** is a machine for taking photographs, making films or videos.

camp *noun* **camps**
A **camp** is a group of tents or huts where people live, usually for a short time.

camp *verb* **camps, camping, camped**
To **camp** means to live or stay in a camp.

candle *noun* **candles**
A **candle** is a stick of wax with a string or wick through the centre which is lit to give light.

cannon *noun* **cannons**
A **cannon** is a big, heavy gun which fires heavy, metal balls.

canoe *noun* **canoes**
A **canoe** is a light, narrow boat with pointed ends which is moved using paddles.

capital *noun* **capitals**
1. A **capital** is the most important town or city in a country.
2. A **capital** is a large letter, such as A, B, C used at the beginning of names and sentences.

captain *noun* **captains**
1. A **captain** is a leader in charge of a team.
2. A **captain** is an officer in the army, navy or air force.

capture *verb* **captures, capturing, captured**
To **capture** means to take something by force or someone prisoner.

caravan *noun* **caravans**
A **caravan** is a small house on wheels that can be towed by a car.

card *noun* **cards**
1. **Card** is stiff, thick paper.
2. A **card** is a piece of card or plastic with writing or pictures on it, such as a Christmas card or a credit card.

cardboard *noun* **cardboard**
Cardboard is thick card or thick, strong paper.

cardigan *noun* **cardigans**
A **cardigan** is a knitted jacket.

careful *adjective*
Someone who does things safely, well or with care is **careful**.

Dictionary fun

Which word describes Edinburgh, Dublin, Ottawa and Canberra? (Clue: look in an atlas.) **?** **?** ? ?

careless *adjective*
Someone who is thoughtless or not careful is **careless**.

carnival *noun* **carnivals**
A **carnival** is a festival usually with a procession of people in fancy dress.

carpet *noun* **carpets**
A **carpet** is a thick, soft cover for the floor.

carrot *noun* **carrots**
A **carrot** is a long, orange vegetable.

carry *verb* **carries, carrying, carried**
To **carry** means to lift and move someone or something from one place to another.

cart *noun* **carts**
A **cart** is a container on wheels, usually pulled by a horse or a person.

carton *noun* **cartons**
A **carton** is a cardboard or plastic box.

cartoon *noun* **cartoons**
1. A **cartoon** is a film made from drawings instead of using actors.
2. A **cartoon** is an amusing drawing.

case *noun* **cases**
A **case** is a bag or container for carrying or keeping things in.

cash *noun*
Cash is coins or paper money.

cassette *noun* **cassettes**
A **cassette** is a plastic case with a tape inside it for playing or recording.

castle *noun* **castles**
A **castle** is a large, strong building with thick, stone walls.

cat *noun* **cats**
A **cat** is a small, furry animal often kept as a pet.

catch *verb* **catches, catching, caught**
1. To **catch** means to capture someone.
2. To **catch** means to get hold of something and stop it from falling.
3. To **catch** means to get an illness.

caterpillar *noun* **caterpillars**
A **caterpillar** is a long, thin, creeping creature that turns into a butterfly or moth.

cathedral *noun* **cathedrals**
A **cathedral** is a large, important church.

cauliflower *noun* **cauliflowers**
A **cauliflower** is a vegetable with a hard, white flower that is eaten.

cave *noun* **caves**
A **cave** is a big hole under the ground or in a mountain or cliff.

ceiling *noun* **ceilings**
A **ceiling** is the roof of a room.

cement *noun*
Cement is a grey powder used to make concrete and mortar for building.

centipede *noun* **centipedes**
A **centipede** is a small, long, creeping creature with many tiny legs.

centre *noun* **centres**
A **centre** is the middle of something.

century *noun* **centuries**
A **century** is 100 years.

cereal *noun* **cereals**
1. A **cereal** is a grain, such as wheat, grown on farms and used as food.
2. A **cereal** is a food eaten at breakfast and made from cereals.

certain *adjective*
1. Someone who is sure of something is **certain**.
2. A particular but not named person is a **certain** person.

certificate *noun* **certificates**
A **certificate** is a piece of paper which states that something has been achieved.

chain *noun* **chains**
A **chain** is a row of linked, metal rings.

chair *noun* **chairs**
A **chair** is a seat with a back for one person to sit on.

chalk *noun* **chalks**
1. **Chalk** is a soft, white rock.
2. A **chalk** is a soft, usually white, stick used for writing and drawing.

Dictionary fun

Which words (on this page) begin with an **s** sound?

? **?** ? ?

champion *noun* **champions**
A **champion** is someone or something that wins a competition or sport.

chance *noun* **chances**
1. A **chance** is something that has not been planned, or an accident.
2. A **chance** is an opportunity to do something.

change *noun* **changes**
1. A **change** is something different from usual.
2. **Change** is money given back to a person who gave too much to pay for something.

change *verb* **changes, changing, changed**
1. To **change** means to become or make different.
2. To **change** means to give something in return for something else.

channel *noun* **channels**
1. A **channel** is a narrow, open stretch that water flows through.
2. A **channel** is a television or radio station.

chapter *noun* **chapters**
A **chapter** is a section of a book.

character *noun* **characters**
1. A **character** is a person in a story or play.
2. A **character** is the kind of person someone is.

charge *verb* **charges, charging, charged**
1. To **charge** means to ask a given price for something.
2. To **charge** means to rush forwards or to attack.

chart *noun* **charts**
1. A **chart** is a large sheet of paper with information or a drawing on it.
2. A **chart** is a map used by sailors.

chase *verb* **chases, chasing, chased**
To **chase** means to run after and try to catch someone or something.

cheap *adjective*
Something that does not cost very much or costs less than usual is **cheap**.

cheat *verb* **cheats, cheating, cheated**
To **cheat** means to break the rules in order to do better in a game or test.

check *noun* **checks**
A **check** is a pattern of coloured squares.

check *verb* **checks, checking, checked**
To **check** means to make sure that something is working properly or is correct.

checkout *noun* **checkouts**
A **checkout** is the counter in a shop where a person pays for the goods.

cheek *noun* **cheeks**
A **cheek** is the side of the face below the eye.

cheer *verb* **cheers, cheering, cheered**
To **cheer** means to shout in a pleasing way to encourage someone.

cheerful *adjective*
Someone who is happy is **cheerful**.

cheese *noun* **cheeses**
Cheese is a solid food made by stirring milk and pressing what is produced.

cherry *noun* **cherries**
A **cherry** is a small red or black fruit.

chess *noun*
Chess is a game for two people played on a board of black and white squares.

chest *noun* **chests**
1. A **chest** is a large, strong box with a lid.
2. A **chest** is the front part of the body between the neck and the waist.

chew *verb* **chews, chewing, chewed**
To **chew** means to bite food into tiny pieces.

chick *noun* **chicks**
A **chick** is a baby bird.

chicken *noun* **chickens**
A **chicken** is a young bird whose meat and eggs are eaten.

child *noun* **children**
1. A **child** is a young girl or boy.
2. A **child** is the son or daughter of someone.

chimney *noun* **chimneys**
A **chimney** is a tall pipe to take away the smoke from a fire.

Dictionary fun

Which word has a silent **h**?

? ? **?** ? ?

a **b c** d e f g h i j k l m n o p q r s t u v w x y z

chimpanzee *noun* chimpanzees
A **chimpanzee** is an African ape, like a large monkey with no tail.

chip *noun* chips
1. A **chip** is a small piece of potato that is fried.
2. A **chip** is a small part used in electronic equipment, such as computers.
3. A **chip** is a very small piece that has broken off something.

chip *verb* chips, chipping, chipped
To **chip** something means to knock it so that a small piece breaks off.

chocolate *noun* chocolates
Chocolate is a sweet food or a drink made from cocoa powder.

choir *noun* choirs
A **choir** is a group of people who sing together.

choose *verb* chooses, choosing, chose, chosen
To **choose** something from a group of things means to take it because it is the one that is wanted or preferred.

chop *noun* chops
A **chop** is a thick slice of meat with a bone along one side.

chop *verb* chops, chopping, chopped
To **chop** means to cut something with a strong force using an axe or a large, sharp knife.

Christmas *noun* Christmases
Christmas is 25 December when the birth of Jesus Christ is celebrated.

church *noun* churches
A **church** is a building where people meet to worship God.

circle *noun* circles
A **circle** is a round, flat shape.

circus *noun* circuses
A **circus** is a show, usually in a large tent, with performing acrobats and clowns and sometimes animals.

city *noun* cities
A **city** is a large, important town.

clap *verb* claps, clapping, clapped
To **clap** means to make a noise by hitting two hands together.

classroom *noun* classrooms
A **classroom** is a room, usually in a school, where a group of students learn together.

claw *noun* claws
A **claw** is a hard, sharp, pointed nail found on the feet of some animals.

clay *noun*
Clay is a sticky kind of earth that becomes very hard when dry and is used for making pottery and bricks.

clean *verb* cleans, cleaning, cleaned
To **clean** means to make something clean.

clean *adjective*
Something that is not dirty is **clean**.

clear *verb* clears, clearing, cleared
To **clear** means to move things out of the way.

clear *adjective*
1. Something that is easy to see, hear or understand is **clear**.
2. Something that is easy to see through is **clear**.
3. Something that has nothing in the way is **clear**.

clever *adjective*
Someone who can learn things very easily or do things skilfully is **clever**.

click *verb* clicks, clicking, clicked
To **click** means to make a short, sharp, clear sound.

cliff *noun* cliffs
A **cliff** is a very steep rock-face, usually at the edge of the sea.

climate *noun* climates
A **climate** is the normal kind of weather a particular region has.

Dictionary fun
Which word is a compound word (can be split into smaller words)?

? **?** ? ?

climb *verb* **climbs, climbing, climbed**
To **climb** means to go up something, such as a ladder or a hill.

cling *verb* **clings, clinging, clung**
To **cling** means to hold on tightly to someone or something.

clinic *noun* **clinics**
A **clinic** is a place like a hospital where people go if they are ill or hurt.

clip *noun* **clips**
A **clip** is a fastener for holding things together, such as papers or hair.

clip *verb* **clips, clipping, clipped**
1. To **clip** means to cut something with scissors or shears.
2. To **clip** something means to fasten it with a clip.

cloak *noun* **cloaks**
A **cloak** is a loose coat with no sleeves which hangs from the shoulders.

clock *noun* **clocks**
A **clock** is a machine for measuring and showing the time.

close *verb* **closes, closing, closed**
To **close** means to shut or to end.

close *adjective*
1. Something that is very near is **close**.
2. When someone looks very carefully or thoroughly, that person has a **close** look.

cloth *noun* **cloths**
1. **Cloth** is material used for making things like clothes or bedding.
2. A **cloth** is a piece of cloth used to cover things or clean things.

clothes *noun*
Clothes are things that are worn to cover the body or to keep warm.

cloud *noun* **clouds**
1. A **cloud** is a white or grey mass of tiny drops of water that floats in the sky.
2. A **cloud** is a mass of smoke or dust that looks like a cloud.

clown *noun* **clowns**
A **clown** is someone in a circus who wears funny clothes and does tricks to make people laugh.

club *noun* **clubs**
1. A **club** is a heavy stick used as a weapon or in some games.
2. A **club** is a group of people with the same interest who meet together.
3. A **club** is a playing card with a black clover leaf on it.

clumsy *adjective*
Someone who often drops things or knocks things over is **clumsy**.

coal *noun* **coals**
Coal is a black rock that can be burned.

coast *noun* **coasts**
A **coast** is the land very near to, and on the edge of, the sea.

cobweb *noun* **cobwebs**
A **cobweb** is a very fine, sticky net spun by a spider to catch insects for food.

cocoa *noun*
Cocoa is a brown powder made from crushed seeds and used to add chocolate flavour to food and drinks.

coconut *noun* **coconuts**
A **coconut** is a large, round, brown nut which grows on a palm tree and has a white flesh and milky juice inside it.

code *noun* **codes**
1. A **code** is a set of rules.
2. A **code** is a set of signs or letters for sending secret messages.

coffee *noun*
Coffee is a brown powder made from crushed, roasted coffee beans that is used to make drinks.

coin *noun* **coins**
A **coin** is a piece of money made of metal.

cold *noun* **colds**
A **cold** is an illness that makes a person cough and sneeze.

cold *adjective*
Someone who is not warm or something that has not been heated is **cold**.

Dictionary fun
Which word has three syllables?

? **?** ? ?

collar *noun* **collars**
1. A **collar** is the part of a piece of clothing that goes round the neck.
2. A **collar** is a band or strap that goes round the neck of an animal.

collect *verb* **collects, collecting, collected**
1. To **collect** means to gather things together in one place.
2. To **collect** means to go and fetch someone or something.

collection *noun* **collections**
A **collection** is a group of things that have been collected.

college *noun* **colleges**
A **college** is a place like a school where people who have finished school go to learn more.

comb *noun* **combs**
A **comb** is a strip with a row of teeth along it, used for keeping the hair tidy.

comb *verb* **combs, combing, combed**
To **comb** means to tidy the hair with a comb.

comfortable *adjective*
Something that is pleasant to use, to sit on or to wear is **comfortable**.

comic *noun* **comics**
A **comic** is a paper with stories told mainly in pictures.

comic *adjective*
Something or someone that is funny is **comic**.

comma *noun* **commas**
A **comma** is a punctuation mark like this , .

common *noun* **commons**
A **common** is an open piece of land for the use of anyone.

common *adjective*
Something that is ordinary or usual is **common**.

compare *verb* **compares, comparing, compared**
To **compare** means to see how similar two or more things are.

compass *noun* **compasses**
A **compass** is an instrument with a needle which always points north.

competition *noun* **competitions**
A **competition** is a game or contest usually with a prize for the winner.

complain *verb* **complains, complaining, complained**
To **complain** means to say that something is not right or not as is wanted.

complete *verb* **completes, completing, completed**
To **complete** something means to finish it.

complete *adjective*
Something that is finished or has all its parts is **complete**.

computer *noun* **computers**
A **computer** is an electronic machine which can solve problems and store information.

concentrate *verb* **concentrates, concentrating, concentrated**
To **concentrate** means to think very hard about what is being done.

concert *noun* **concerts**
A **concert** is a performance where music is played.

concrete *noun*
Concrete is a mixture of cement and sand that sets very hard and is used for building.

cone *noun* **cones**
1. A **cone** is a solid shape like an ice-cream cone.
2. A **cone** is a case containing the seed on an evergreen tree.

confuse *verb* **confuses, confusing, confused**
To **confuse** means to mix up or to muddle.

connect *verb* **connects, connecting, connected**
To **connect** means to join together.

consist *verb* **consists, consisting, consisted**
To **consist** means to be made up of certain things.

consonant *noun* **consonants**
A **consonant** is any letter of the alphabet except the five vowels (a, e, i, o, u).

Dictionary fun
Which word can be connected to the words **disk**, **program** and **screen**?

?

construct *verb* **constructs, constructing, constructed**
To **construct** means to build.

contain *verb* **contains, containing, contained**
To **contain** means to have or to hold something inside.

container *noun* **containers**
A **container** is something that can hold things inside it.

continent *noun* **continents**
A **continent** is one of the seven very large areas of land in the world.

continue *verb* **continues, continuing, continued**
To **continue** means to go on doing something.

control *verb* **controls, controlling, controlled**
To **control** means to make someone or something do what is wanted.

conversation *noun* **conversations**
A **conversation** is when two or more people talk and listen to each other.

cook *noun* **cooks**
A **cook** is someone whose job is to prepare food.

cook *verb* **cooks, cooking, cooked**
To **cook** means to prepare food for eating by heating it in different ways.

cooker *noun* **cookers**
A **cooker** is an oven used for cooking food.

cool *adjective*
Something that is fairly cold or not warm is **cool**.

copper *noun* **copper**
Copper is a reddish-brown metal used to make coins and pipes.

copy *verb* **copies, copying, copied**
1. To **copy** means to write or draw exactly what has already been written or drawn.
2. To **copy** means to do exactly the same as someone else.

cork *noun* **corks**
1. **Cork** is the bark of a special kind of tree.
2. A **cork** is a piece of cork used to close a bottle.

corn *noun* **corn**
Corn is a plant that has ears or cobs.

corner *noun* **corners**
A **corner** is the point where two roads, walls or lines meet.

correct *adjective*
Something that has no mistakes or is completely right is **correct**.

corridor *noun* **corridors**
A **corridor** is a narrow passage with doors leading to different rooms or compartments along it.

cost *noun* **costs**
A **cost** is the price of something.

costume *noun* **costumes**
1. A **costume** is the clothes worn by an actor in a play.
2. A **costume** is clothes like those worn a long time ago.

cottage *noun* **cottages**
A **cottage** is a small house.

cotton *noun*
Cotton is thread or cloth made from the cotton plant.

cough *noun* **coughs**
A **cough** is a sudden, loud noise made to get rid of something or stop a tickling feeling in the throat.

could *verb*
Could means that someone was able or may be able to do something.

count *verb* **counts, counting, counted**
To **count** means to say the numbers in order.

counter *noun* **counters**
1. A **counter** is a long, narrow table where people are served in a shop, bank or café.
2. A **counter** is a small disc used to keep the score in some games.

country *noun* **countries**
A **country** is a place where people live, such as Australia, Canada, England or Ireland.

couple *noun* **couples**
A **couple** is two of something.

Dictionary fun

Which two words can you change to **wore** by changing two letters?

? **?** ? ?

course *noun* **courses**
1. A **course** is a series or group of lessons.
2. A **course** is an area of land on which certain sports take place, such as golf.
3. A **course** is the direction something or someone takes.

cousin *noun* **cousins**
A **cousin** is the child of someone's aunt or uncle.

cover *noun* **covers**
A **cover** is something that is put over things.

cover *verb* **covers, covering, covered**
To **cover** means to put one thing over another to hide it, protect it or keep it warm.

cow *noun* **cows**
A **cow** is a female animal kept on farms for its milk and meat.

crab *noun* **crabs**
A **crab** is a shellfish with eight legs and two pincers.

crack *noun* **cracks**
A **crack** is a narrow line in something where it has broken but not fallen apart.

crack *verb* **cracks, cracking, cracked**
To **crack** means to get or make a crack which often makes a sudden noise.

cracker *noun* **crackers**
1. A **cracker** is a paper tube with a toy and paper hat inside, which bangs when the ends are pulled.
2. A **cracker** is a thin, dry biscuit.

cradle *noun* **cradles**
A **cradle** is a baby's bed.

crane *noun* **cranes**
1. A **crane** is a large machine for lifting very heavy objects.
2. A **crane** is a large bird with long legs and a long neck.

crash *noun* **crashes**
A **crash** is the loud noise made when one thing hits into or falls onto another.

crash *verb* **crashes, crashing, crashed**
To **crash** means to hit something suddenly, making a loud noise.

crawl *noun*
The **crawl** is a swimming stroke.

crawl *verb* **crawls, crawling, crawled**
To **crawl** means to move slowly, often on hands and knees.

crayon *noun* **crayons**
A **crayon** is a coloured pencil.

cream *noun* **cream**
1. **Cream** is the thick part on the top of milk that can be made into butter.
2. **Cream** is something that looks like cream and that is rubbed into the skin.

creature *noun* **creatures**
A **creature** is any animal.

creek *noun* **creeks**
A **creek** is a small stream.

crew *noun* **crews**
A **crew** is the group of people who work on a ship or plane.

cricket *noun* **crickets**
1. **Cricket** is an outdoor game played by two teams with a ball, bats and wickets.
2. A **cricket** is an insect like a grasshopper which makes a piercing noise.

cried *verb*
This is the past tense of the verb 'to cry' (see **cry**).

criminal *noun* **criminals**
A **criminal** is someone who has broken the law.

crocodile *noun* **crocodiles**
A **crocodile** is a long, large reptile with sharp teeth that lives in rivers.

crooked *adjective*
Something that is not straight is **crooked**.

crop *noun* **crops**
A **crop** is a plant grown for food.

crop *verb* **crops, cropping, cropped**
To **crop** means to cut something, such as hair or grass, very short.

Dictionary fun
To which word could you add an **s** at the beginning to make a noun that means 'loud cry'?
? ? ? ?

cross *noun* **crosses**
A **cross** is a mark or a shape like this + or this x.

cross *verb* **crosses, crossing, crossed**
To **cross** means to move from one side of something to the other.

cross *adjective*
Someone who is angry is **cross**.

crowd *noun* **crowds**
A **crowd** is a large number of people in one place.

crown *noun* **crowns**
A **crown** is a gold ring worn on the head by a king or queen.

cruel *adjective*
Someone who is very unkind is **cruel**.

crumb *noun* **crumbs**
A **crumb** is a tiny piece of bread or cake.

crust *noun* **crusts**
A **crust** is the hard outer covering of a loaf of bread or a pie.

cry *verb* **cries, crying, cried**
1. To **cry** means to become upset so that tears fall from the eyes.
2. To **cry** means to shout.

crystal *noun* **crystals**
A **crystal** is a piece of hard material that looks like glass.

cub *noun* **cubs**
A **cub** is a young animal, such as a lion or fox.

cube *noun* **cubes**
A **cube** is a solid shape with six square sides. Dice are cubes.

cuckoo *noun* **cuckoos**
A **cuckoo** is a bird that lays its eggs in another bird's nest.

cucumber *noun* **cucumbers**
A **cucumber** is a long, green vegetable used in salads.

cup *noun* **cups**
1. A **cup** is a small bowl with a handle for drinking from.
2. A **cup** is a gold or silver bowl given as a prize.

cupboard *noun* **cupboards**
A **cupboard** is a piece of furniture or space in a wall with doors, for storing things.

cure *verb* **cures, curing, cured**
To **cure** means to make well again or stop a problem.

curious *adjective*
1. Someone who wants to find out anything new is **curious**.
2. Something that is unusual or strange is **curious**.

curl *noun* **curls**
A **curl** is a piece of hair that twists into a curve.

curl *verb* **curls, curling, curled**
To **curl** means to twist into the shape of a curl.

currant *noun* **currants**
A **currant** is a small, dried, black grape.

current *noun* **currents**
A **current** is a stream or flow of air, water or electricity.

curtain *noun* **curtains**
A **curtain** is a piece of cloth hung at a window, door or stage to cover it.

curve *noun* **curves**
A **curve** is a line which bends smoothly so there are no sharp corners.

cushion *noun* **cushions**
A **cushion** is a bag filled with feathers or a soft material for sitting on.

customs *noun* **customs**
Customs is the place where luggage is examined when someone comes into a country.

cut *noun* **cuts**
A **cut** is a small wound in the skin made by something sharp.

cut *verb* **cuts, cutting, cut**
To **cut** means to use scissors or a knife to divide something into pieces.

cycle *verb* **cycles, cycling, cycled**
To **cycle** means to ride a bicycle.

Dictionary fun
Which word is a compound word (can be split into smaller words)?

? **?** ? ?

Dd

daily *adjective and adverb*
Something that happens every day happens **daily**.

dairy *noun* **dairies**
A **dairy** is a place where milk is made into butter and cheese.

dam *noun* **dams**
A **dam** is a strong wall built across a river to hold the water back.

damage *verb* **damages, damaging, damaged**
To **damage** something means to break or spoil it.

damp *adjective*
Something that is slightly wet is **damp**.

dance *verb* **dances, dancing, danced**
To **dance** means to move in time to music.

dancer *noun* **dancers**
A **dancer** is a person who dances.

danger *noun* **dangers**
1. A **danger** is something that could harm someone.
2. A **danger** is the chance of being harmed.

dangerous *adjective*
Something that could kill or hurt someone is **dangerous**.

dark *adjective*
Something that is not light in colour or has very little light is **dark**.

dart *noun* **darts**
A **dart** is a short arrow that is thrown at a target in a game.

dart *verb* **darts, darting, darted**
To **dart** means to move suddenly and quickly.

date *noun* **dates**
1. A **date** is the day, month and year when something happens.
2. A **date** is a soft, brown, sweet fruit that grows on a palm tree.

daughter *noun* **daughters**
A **daughter** is a girl or woman who is the child of someone.

dawn *noun* **dawns**
Dawn is the first light of day when the sun rises.

day *noun* **days**
1. A **day** is a period of 24 hours from one midnight to the next midnight.
2. **Day** is the part of the day when it is light.

dazzle *verb* **dazzles, dazzling, dazzled**
To **dazzle** means to shine so brightly that people cannot see properly.

dead *adjective*
Something that is not alive is **dead**.

deaf *adjective*
Someone who cannot hear is **deaf**.

dear *adjective*
1. Someone who is loved is **dear**.
2. Something that costs a lot is **dear**.
3. A letter is often started with 'Dear ...'.

death *noun* **deaths**
A **death** is the time when life ends.

deceive *verb* **deceives, deceiving, deceived**
To **deceive** means to make someone believe something that is not true.

decide *verb* **decides, deciding, decided**
To **decide** means to make up your mind about something or to choose it.

deck *noun* **decks**
A **deck** is one of the floors in a ship or bus.

decorate *verb* **decorates, decorating, decorated**
To **decorate** means to make something look pretty or colourful.

Dictionary fun
Which word on this page sounds the same as a word on page 24 but is spelled differently?

? **?** **?**

deed *noun* **deeds**
A **deed** is something that someone has done.

deep *adjective*
Something that goes a long way down from the top is **deep**.

deer *noun* **deer**
A **deer** is a timid, wild animal. The male deer (stag) has antlers.

defeat *verb* **defeats, defeating, defeated**
To **defeat** means to beat someone in a game or battle.

defend *verb* **defends, defending, defended**
To **defend** means to guard, protect or keep someone or something safe.

degree *noun* **degrees**
A **degree** is a measurement for temperature and for angles.

delicious *adjective*
Something that tastes or smells very pleasant is **delicious**.

deliver *verb* **delivers, delivering, delivered**
To **deliver** means to take something to wherever it has to go.

dent *verb* **dents, denting, dented**
To **dent** means to hit something so that a hollow is made in it.

dentist *noun* **dentists**
A **dentist** is someone whose job is to look after people's teeth.

deposit *noun* **deposits**
1. A **deposit** is the first payment for something.
2. A **deposit** is the money put into a bank account.

depth *noun* **depths**
A **depth** is a measurement from top to bottom or front to back of something.

describe *verb* **describes, describing, described**
To **describe** means to explain what someone or something is like.

description *noun* **descriptions**
A **description** is the words that explain what someone or something is like.

desert *noun* **deserts**
A **desert** is a large, dry, usually sandy area of land where little can grow.

deserve *verb* **deserves, deserving, deserved**
To **deserve** means to be good enough to receive a reward or to be bad enough to receive a punishment.

desk *noun* **desks**
A **desk** is a kind of table where someone reads or writes.

destroy *verb* **destroys, destroying, destroyed**
To **destroy** means to damage something so badly that it cannot be used or live again.

dew *noun* **dew**
Dew is tiny drops of water that form on outdoor things during the night.

diagonal *noun* **diagonals**
A **diagonal** is a straight line across a shape from one corner to the opposite corner.

diagram *noun* **diagrams**
A **diagram** is a picture or plan that explains something.

dial *noun* **dials**
A **dial** is a circle with numbers or letters round it, such as on a clock.

diamond *noun* **diamonds**
1. A **diamond** is a very hard, sparkling, precious stone that looks like glass.
2. A **diamond** is a shape with four equal sides which is not a square.
3. A **diamond** is a playing-card with a red shape like a diamond on it.

diary *noun* **diaries**
A **diary** is a book in which events that happen each day are written down.

Dictionary fun

Which word is the same forwards and backwards?

? **?** ? ?

dice *noun*
This is the plural of the noun 'die' (see **die**).

dictionary *noun* **dictionaries**
A **dictionary** is a book in which the meaning of words, listed in alphabetical order, are explained.

die *noun* **dice**
A **die** is a small cube used in games. The numbers 1 to 6 are printed on its 6 sides.

die *verb* **dies, dying, died**
To **die** means to stop living.

difference *noun* **differences**
A **difference** is the way in which one thing is not like another.

different *adjective*
Someone or something that is not like another is **different**.

difficult *adjective*
Something that is not easy is **difficult**.

dim *adjective*
Something that is not bright is **dim**.

dining *adjective*
Someone who is eating is **dining**.

dinner *noun* **dinners**
Dinner is the main meal of the day.

dinosaur *noun* **dinosaurs**
A **dinosaur** is an animal that lived millions of years ago.

direction *noun* **directions**
A **direction** is the way to go to get somewhere.

dirt *noun* **dirt**
Dirt is mud or dust.

disagree *verb* **disagrees, disagreeing, disagreed**
To **disagree** means to think that you are right and someone else is wrong, or to quarrel with someone.

disappear *verb* **disappears, disappearing, disappeared**
To **disappear** means to go away so that the person or object cannot be seen.

disappoint *verb* **disappoints, disappointing, disappointed**
To **disappoint** means to make someone sad by not doing what was hoped for.

disaster *noun* **disasters**
A **disaster** is a serious accident that happens suddenly.

discover *verb* **discovers, discovering, discovered**
To **discover** means to find something or to find out about something.

discuss *verb* **discusses, discussing, discussed**
To **discuss** means to talk about something with other people.

disease *noun* **diseases**
A **disease** is an illness.

dish *noun* **dishes**
1. A **dish** is a shallow bowl for cooking or serving food.
2. A **dish** is a kind of aerial for receiving television broadcasts.

dishonest *adjective*
Someone who does not tell the truth is **dishonest**.

dishwasher *noun* **dishwashers**
A **dishwasher** is a machine for washing all kinds of dishes.

dislike *verb* **dislikes, disliking, disliked**
To **dislike** means not to like someone or something.

disk *noun* **disks**
1. A **disk** is any object that is flat and round.
2. A **disk** plays music on a CD-player or a record-player.
3. A **disk** stores information for a computer.

Dictionary fun

Which words have the prefix dis- which reverses the meaning?

? ? ? ?

disobey *verb* **disobeys, disobeying, disobeyed**
To **disobey** means to break the rules.

distance *noun* **distances**
A **distance** is the space between two places.

disturb *verb* **disturbs, disturbing, disturbed**
1. To **disturb** means to spoil someone's rest or thought.
2. To **disturb** means to move something from its place.

ditch *noun* **ditches**
A **ditch** is a long, narrow trench, dug to drain water from land.

dive *verb* **dives, diving, dived**
To **dive** means to jump head first into the water.

divide *verb* **divides, dividing, divides**
1. To **divide** means to separate or to share something into parts.
2. To **divide** means to see how many times one number goes into another.

doctor *noun* **doctors**
A **doctor** is a person whose job is to try to make sick people better.

dog *noun* **dogs**
A **dog** is an animal that is often kept as a pet.

doll *noun* **dolls**
A **doll** is a toy in the shape of a baby or person.

dollar *noun* **dollars**
A **dollar** is an amount of money used in the USA, Canada, Australia and other countries.

dolphin *noun* **dolphins**
A **dolphin** is an animal like a small whale that lives in the sea.

donkey *noun* **donkeys**
A **donkey** is an animal like a small horse with long ears.

door *noun* **doors**
A **door** is something that opens and closes to allow people to get into or out of a building, room or cupboard.

doubt *verb* **doubts, doubting, doubted**
To **doubt** means to be unsure about something.

dough *noun* **dough**
Dough is a mixture of flour and water used for making bread and cakes.

down *noun* **down**
Down is the soft, fluffy feathers on birds.

down *preposition and adverb*
When someone or something goes from a higher to a lower place, it goes **down**. *She fell down the stairs.*

downstairs *adjective and adverb*
Something that is on a lower or ground floor of a building is **downstairs**.

dozen *noun* **dozens**
A **dozen** is a set or group of twelve things.

drag *verb* **drags, dragging, dragged**
To **drag** means to pull something along.

dragon *noun* **dragons**
A **dragon** is a fire-breathing monster in stories.

drain *noun* **drains**
A **drain** is a pipe for taking away water or sewage.

drain *verb* **drains, draining, drained**
To **drain** means to take away or let water run off something.

drank *verb*
This is the past tense of the verb 'to drink'(see **drink**).

draught *noun* **draughts**
A **draught** is cold air that blows indoors.

draw *verb* **draws, drawing, drew**
1. To **draw** means to make a picture with a pen or pencils.
2. To **draw** means to finish a game with each side scoring the same.

Dictionary fun

What sound does the **gh** in draught make? Which other word has this sound in it? **? ? ? ?**

drawbridge *noun* **drawbridges**
A **drawbridge** is a bridge over a moat round a castle that can be pulled up to stop people attacking the castle.

drawer *noun* **drawers**
A **drawer** is a tray that slides into a piece of furniture.

drawing *noun* **drawings**
A **drawing** is a picture or diagram drawn with pens or pencils.

dreadful *adjective*
Something that is very bad is **dreadful**.

dream *verb* **dreams, dreaming, dreamed**
To **dream** means to seem to see and hear things when asleep.

dress *noun* **dresses**
A **dress** is a piece of clothing that has a top joined to a skirt.

dress *verb* **dresses, dressing, dressed**
To **dress** means to put clothes on.

drier *noun* **driers**
A **drier** is a machine in which washing is dried.

drift *verb* **drifts, drifting, drifted**
To **drift** means to be carried along gently by a current of air or water.

drill *noun* **drills**
1. A **drill** is a tool for making holes.
2. A **drill** is a set of exercises done by soldiers when training.

drink *verb* **drinks, drinking, drank, drunk**
To **drink** means to swallow any kind of liquid.

drip *verb* **drips, dripping, dripped**
To **drip** means to fall in drops of liquid.

drive *verb* **drives, driving, drove, driven**
To **drive** means to make something move`, such as a vehicle, machine or animal.

driver *noun* **drivers**
A **driver** is the person who drives the vehicle, machine or animal.

drop *noun* **drops**
A **drop** is a very small amount of liquid.

drop *verb* **drops, dropping, dropped**
To **drop** means to let something fall.

drown *verb* **drowns, drowning, drowned**
To **drown** means to die by not being able to breathe under water.

drum *noun* **drums**
A **drum** is a musical instrument that is banged with sticks.

dry *adjective*
Something that is not wet is **dry**.

duck *noun* **ducks**
A **duck** is a bird that lives near water and makes a quacking noise.

duck *verb* **ducks, ducking, ducked**
To **duck** means to bend down quickly to avoid being hit by something.

duet *noun* **duets**
A **duet** is a piece of music for two people to play or sing.

dull *adjective*
Something that is not interesting or is not bright is **dull**.

dungeon *noun* **dungeons**
A **dungeon** is an underground prison in a castle.

during *preposition*
When something happens while something else is happening, it is happening **during** it. *I scored five runs during the match.*

dust *noun* **dust**
Dust is powdery, dry dirt.

dust *verb* **dusts, dusting, dusted**
To **dust** means to clean away dust.

duster *noun* **dusters**
A **duster** is a cloth used for cleaning away dust.

dwarf *noun* **dwarfs**
A **dwarf** is a very small person or thing.

Dictionary fun
Which word is the opposite of wet?

? **?** ? ?

a b c d e f g h i j k l m n o p q r s t u v w x y z

Ee

each *adjective and pronoun*
Each means every single one or thing.

eager *adjective*
Someone who wants to do something very much is **eager**.

eagle *noun* **eagles**
An **eagle** is a very large bird that eats other animals.

ear *noun* **ears**
An **ear** is on each side of the head and is used for hearing.

early *adjective and adverb*
1. Something that is near the beginning is **early**.
2. Something that happens sooner than expected happens **early**.

earn *verb* **earns, earning, earned**
To **earn** means to get something, often money, as payment for work done.

earring *noun* **earrings**
An **earring** is a piece of jewellery worn on the ear.

Earth *noun*
The **Earth** is the planet we live on.

earth *noun*
Soil is **earth**.

earthquake *noun* **earthquakes**
An **earthquake** is the time when the ground suddenly shakes and can split open.

easel *noun* **easels**
An **easel** is a stand for holding a picture or blackboard.

east *noun*
East is one of the points of the compass and is the direction from which the sun rises.

Easter *noun*
Easter is the day on which many people believe that Jesus Christ rose from the dead.

easy *adjective*
Something that can be done without any difficulty is **easy**.

eat *verb* **eats, eating, ate, eaten**
To **eat** means to put food into the mouth, bite it and swallow it.

echo *noun* **echoes**
An **echo** is a sound which is heard again by bouncing back off something solid, such as the wall of a cave.

eclipse *noun* **eclipses**
An **eclipse** is the time when the Moon gets between the Earth and the Sun and blocks out the Sun's light or the Sun gets between the Earth and the Moon and blocks out the Moon's light.

edge *noun* **edges**
An **edge** is the end or side of something.

education *noun*
Education is the teaching and learning that takes place in a school or college.

effect *noun* **effects**
An **effect** is the result of something happening.

effort *noun* **efforts**
An **effort** is the hard work someone is doing or trying to do.

egg *noun* **eggs**
An **egg** is an oval or round object laid by a bird, fish, insect or reptile in which the young start to grow. Some eggs can be eaten as food.

either *adjective and pronoun*
Either is one or the other of two things or people.

elastic *noun*
Elastic is a material which can stretch and then go back to its original size.

Dictionary fun

Which two words begin with a capital letter? Why?

? ? ? ?

a b c d **e** f g h i j k l m n o p q r s t u v w x y z

elbow *noun* **elbows**
An **elbow** is the part in the middle of the arm which bends.

electric *adjective*
Something that uses electricity to work is **electric**.

electrician *noun* **electricians**
An **electrician** is a person whose job is to work with electrical machines and wires.

electricity *noun* **electricity**
Electricity is a form of power or energy which produces light and heat and makes machines work.

elephant *noun*
elephants
An **elephant** is a very large, grey animal with tusks and a long trunk.

elf *noun* **elves**
An **elf** is a small fairy.

emerald *noun* **emeralds**
An **emerald** is a green, precious stone used in jewellery.

emergency *noun* **emergencies**
An **emergency** is something very dangerous or a crisis that happens suddenly.

empty *adjective*
Something that has nothing in it is **empty**.

emu *noun* **emus**
An **emu** is a large, Australian bird that cannot fly.

end *noun* **ends**
An **end** is the last part of something.

end *verb* **ends, ending, ended**
To **end** means to finish.

enemy *noun* **enemies**
1. An **enemy** is someone who hates and wants to harm someone else.
2. An **enemy** is the people fighting on the other side in a war.

energetic *adjective*
Someone who has the strength or energy to do a lot of things is **energetic**.

energy *noun* **energies**
Energy is the strength or power to do things.

engine *noun*
engines
An **engine** is a machine that provides power to move things.

engineer *noun* **engineers**
An **engineer** is a person whose job is to design and make machines, roads and bridges.

engineering *noun* **engineering**
Engineering is the designing, building and repairing of things like machines, roads and bridges.

English *adjective*
English is a language.

enjoy *verb* **enjoys, enjoying, enjoyed**
To **enjoy** means to like doing something.

enormous *adjective*
Something that is very big is **enormous**.

enough *adjective, noun and adverb*
Someone who has as much of something as is needed has **enough**.

enter *verb* **enters, entering, entered**
1. To **enter** means to go or come in.
2. To **enter** means to take part in a race, competition or examination.

entertain *verb* **entertains, entertaining, entertained**
To **entertain** means to amuse someone by giving that person pleasure.

entertainment *noun* **entertainments**
An **entertainment** is something that entertains or amuses people, such as a circus or play.

entrance *noun*
entrances
An **entrance** is a way in.

Dictionary fun
Which is the second most spoken language in the world?

? **?** ? ?

envelope *noun* **envelopes**
An **envelope** is a cover with a flap to hold a letter or other paper.

environment *noun* **environments**
An **environment** is all the surroundings that affect the way something or someone lives.

envy *noun*
Envy is something that is felt when one person wants what another person has.

equal *adjective*
Something that is the same size, amount or value as something else is **equal** to it.

equator *noun*
The **equator** is an imaginary line round the middle of the earth.

equipment *noun*
Equipment is the things needed to do a particular job.

error *noun* **errors**
An **error** is a mistake.

escape *verb* **escapes, escaping, escaped**
To **escape** means to get out or to get away.

especially *adverb*
When something is wanted more than anything, it is wanted **especially**.

estate *noun* **estates**
An **estate** is a large area of land on which houses or factories are built.

even *adjective*
1. Something that is smooth or level or equal is **even**.
2. A number that can be divided exactly by two is **even**.

evening *noun* **evenings**
Evening is the time of day between the end of the afternoon and night.

event *noun* **events**
An **event** is something important that happens.

ever *adverb*
1. When something may have happened at any time, it may **ever** have happened. *Have you ever done that?*
2. When something has always happened, it has **ever** happened. *They lived happily ever after.*

every *adjective*
When each one in a group is considered, **every** one is included.

everybody *pronoun*
Everybody is every person.

everyone *pronoun*
Everyone is every person.

everything *pronoun*
Everything is all things.

everywhere *adverb*
Someone who looks in all places looks **everywhere**.

evil *adjective*
Something or someone who is very wicked is **evil**.

exactly *adverb*
When something has been done perfectly right, it has been done **exactly**.

exam *noun* **exams**
An **exam** is an important test and is short for examination.

examination *noun* **examinations**
An **examination** is an important test.

examine *verb* **examines, examining, examined**
To **examine** means to look at something very carefully.

Dictionary fun

Which word can have its letters moved around to make **live**?

?

a b c d e f g h i j k l m n o p q r s t u v w x y z

example *noun* **examples**
1. An **example** is something that shows what a certain thing is like.
2. An **example** is someone or something that should be copied.

excellent *adjective*
Something that is very good is **excellent**.

except *preposition*
When all apart from certain people do something, all **except** a few do it. *Everyone went to the party except Peter.*

excite *verb* **excites, exciting, excited**
To **excite** means to make someone feel very lively, interested or active.

excuse *noun* **excuses**
An **excuse** is a reason given to explain why someone did something wrong.

excuse *verb* **excuses, excusing, excused**
To **excuse** means to forgive.

exercise *noun* **exercises**

1. An **exercise** is something done to make the body strong and fit.
2. An **exercise** is a piece of work that is done for practice.

exit *noun* **exits**
An **exit** is a way out of a place.

expect *verb* **expects, expecting, expected**
To **expect** means to think that something is going to happen.

expensive *adjective*
Something that costs a great deal of money is **expensive**.

explain *verb* **explains, explaining, explained**
To **explain** means to make something clear so that it is understood.

explanation *noun* **explanations**
An **explanation** is the words used to help people understand something.

explode *verb* **explodes, exploding, exploded**
To **explode** means to go off or burst with a loud bang.

explore *verb* **explores, exploring, explored**
To **explore** means to look carefully round an unknown area.

explorer *noun* **explorers**
An **explorer** is a person who goes to unknown places to see what they are like.

express *noun* **expresses**
An **express** is a fast train.

express *verb* **expresses, expressing, expressed**
To **express** means to talk or write about an idea or a feeling.

expression *noun* **expressions**
An **expression** is the look on someone's face.

extinct *adjective*
When something no longer exists or is no longer active, it is **extinct**.

extra *adjective and adverb*
Something that is more than usual or more than needed is **extra**.

eyebrow *noun* **eyebrows**
An **eyebrow** is the curved line of hair above the eye.

eyelash *noun* **eyelashes**
An **eyelash** is one of the short hairs that grows round the eyelid.

eyelid *noun* **eyelids**
An **eyelid** is the piece of skin that can close over the eye.

eye *noun* **eyes**
An **eye** is one of two parts on a face, used for seeing.

eyesight *noun* **eyesight**
Eyesight is the ability to see.

Dictionary fun
Which word describes Marco Polo, Christopher Columbus and Captain Cook?

? ? ? ?

a b c d e f g h i j k l m n o p q r s t u v w x y z

Ff

fabric *noun* **fabrics**
Fabric is cloth or material.

face *noun* **faces**
1. A **face** is the front part of the head.
2. A **face** is a surface.

face *verb* **faces, facing, faced**
To **face** means to have the front pointing in a certain direction.

fact *noun* **facts**
A **fact** is anything that is known to be true.

factory *noun* **factories**
A **factory** is a building in which things are made by machines.

fade *verb* **fades, fading, faded**
To **fade** means to lose colour or to become quieter.

fail *verb* **fails, failing, failed**
To **fail** means to try to do something but not to be successful.

faint *adjective*
1. Something that is weak or dim is **faint**.
2. Someone who feels dizzy feels **faint**.

faint *verb* **faints, fainting, fainted**
To faint means to feel dizzy and fall over.

fair *noun* **fairs**
A **fair** is an entertainment with rides, games, displays and stalls.

fair *adjective*
1. Something that has a light colour is **fair**.
2. Something or someone who is right or honest is **fair**.

fairy *noun* **fairies**
A **fairy** is a small, magic person in stories.

faithful *adjective*
Someone who is always reliable and loyal is **faithful**.

fall *verb* **falls, falling, fell, fallen**
To **fall** means to come down, sometimes unexpectedly.

false *adjective*
Something that is not true or not real is **false**.

family *noun* **families**
A **family** is a group of people who are closely related, such as parents and their children.

famine *noun* **famines**
A **famine** is a very great shortage of food.

famous *adjective*
Someone or something that is very well known is **famous**.

fan *noun* **fans**
1. A **fan** is a supporter of something, such as a football team.
2. A **fan** is something that blows air to cool people down.

fang *noun* **fangs**
A **fang** is a long, sharp tooth.

fantastic *adjective*
Something that is really good or wonderful is **fantastic**.

far *adjective and adverb*
Something that is a long way away is **far**.

fare *noun* **fares**
A **fare** is the money people pay to travel on a bus, train, ship or plane.

farm *noun* **farms**
A **farm** is an area of land where animals are kept and crops are grown for food.

farmer *noun* **farmers**
A **farmer** is someone who has a farm.

fast *verb* **fasts, fasting, fasted**
To **fast** means to have nothing to eat for a time.

fast *adjective*
1. Something that moves quickly is **fast**.
2. Something that is fixed very firmly is **fast**.

Dictionary fun

Which word becomes **point** by changing two letters?

? ? ? ?

fasten *verb* **fastens, fastening, fastened**
To **fasten** means to fix together.

fat *noun* **fats**
1. **Fat** is the white, greasy part of meat.
2. **Fat** is grease, like butter or margarine, used in cooking.

fat *adjective*
Something that is very thick is **fat**.

father *noun* **fathers**
A **father** is a male parent.

fault *noun* **faults**
A **fault** is a mistake.

favourite *adjective*
Something that is liked the best is **favourite**.

fear *noun* **fears**
A **fear** is what is felt when something frightening, dangerous or painful might happen.

fear *verb* **fears, fearing, feared**
To **fear** means to be frightened of someone or something.

feast *noun* **feasts**
A **feast** is a special, large meal for a lot of people.

feather *noun* **feathers**
A **feather** is one of the soft, light parts that cover a bird's skin.

feeble *adjective*
Someone who is weak is **feeble**.

feed *verb* **feeds, feeding, fed**
1. To **feed** means to give food to.
2. To **feed** means to eat food.

feel *verb* **feels, feeling, felt**
1. To **feel** means to touch something.
2. To **feel** means to think or know something.

feet *noun*
This is the plural of the noun 'foot' (see **foot**).

fell *verb*
This is the past tense of the verb 'to fall' (see **fall**).

female *noun* **females**
A **female** is a person or animal who is, or can become, a mother.

fence *noun* **fences**
A **fence** is a row of posts with wood or wire between them that goes along the edge of a piece of land.

ferry *noun* **ferries**
A **ferry** is a boat that carries people or objects across a river, lake or channel.

festival *noun* **festivals**
A **festival** is a time when people celebrate an event.

fetch *verb* **fetches, fetching, fetched**
To **fetch** means to go and get something and bring it back.

fever *noun* **fevers**
A **fever** is an illness where the person feels very hot.

few *pronoun*
A **few** is a small number of things. *Only a few had engine trouble.*

few *adjective*
When there are not many of something, there are **few**. *Only a few cars had engine trouble.*

fibre *noun* **fibres**
A **fibre** is a very thin thread.

field *noun* **fields**
A **field** is a piece of land with a fence or hedge round it and grass or crops growing in it.

fierce *adjective*
Someone or something that is angry and violent is **fierce**.

fig *noun* **figs**
A **fig** is a small, soft fruit.

Dictionary fun

In which word is the **t** silent?

? ? ? ?

fight *verb* **fights, fighting, fought**
To **fight** means to try to hurt someone in a struggle or in a war.

figure *noun* **figures**
1. A **figure** is the shape of a person's body.
2. A **figure** is a sign used for a number, such as 1, 2 or 3.

fill *verb* **fills, filling, filled**
To **fill** means to make or become full.

film *noun* **films**
1. A **film** is the roll of plastic used in a camera to take photographs.
2. A **film** is moving pictures with sound.

filthy *adjective*
Something that is very dirty is **filthy**.

fin *noun* **fins**
A **fin** is a part of a fish's body that helps it to swim.

final *adjective*
Something that comes last or is at the end is the **final** one.

find *verb* **finds, finding, found**
To **find** something means to come across or discover it.

fine *noun* **fines**
A **fine** is the money that has to be paid for doing something wrong.

fine *adjective*
1. Something that is very thin is **fine**.
2. Something that is very good is **fine**.
3. Weather that is dry and bright is **fine**.

finger *noun* **fingers**
A **finger** is one of the five parts of the body at the end of the hand.

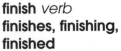

finish *verb* **finishes, finishing, finished**
To **finish** means to come to the end or complete something.

fire *noun* **fires**
A **fire** is the flames and heat that come when something is burning.

fire *verb* **fires, firing, fired**
To **fire** means to shoot a bullet from a gun.

fireplace *noun* **fireplaces**
A **fireplace** is the part of a room where a fire can be lit.

firework *noun* **fireworks**
A **firework** is a tube full of powder, which when lit sends out brightly coloured sparks or bangs.

firm *adjective*
Something that is fixed and solid so that it will not break is **firm**.

fish *noun* **fish or fishes**
A **fish** is an animal with scales that lives and breathes under water.

fish *verb* **fishes, fishing, fished**
To **fish** means to try to catch fish.

fist *noun* **fists**
A **fist** is a hand with the fingers closed tightly onto the palm.

fit *verb* **fits, fitting, fitted**
To **fit** means to be the right size and shape.

fit *adjective*
1. Someone who is healthy is **fit**.
2. Someone or something that is suitable is **fit**.

fix *verb* **fixes, fixing, fixed**
1. To **fix** something means to mend it.
2. To **fix** means to join or fasten something firmly to another object.

flag *noun* **flags**
A **flag** is a piece of cloth, usually with a coloured design on it, belonging to a group or country.

flame *noun* **flames**
A **flame** is a bright, tongue-shaped light from a fire.

flamingo *noun* **flamingos** or **flamingoes**
A **flamingo** is a large, long-legged bird with pink feathers.

Dictionary fun
You have eight of these. What are they?

? **?** ? ?

a b c d e f g h i j k l m n o p q r s t u v w x y z

flap *noun* **flaps**
A **flap** is a piece of material or paper that hangs from one edge of something to cover an opening.

flap *verb* **flaps, flapping, flapped**
To **flap** means to move up and down like a bird's wings when flying.

flash *verb* **flashes, flashing, flashed**
1. To **flash** means to shine a light suddenly.
2. To **flash** means to come into and go out of sight very quickly.

flask *noun* **flasks**
A **flask** is a container for drinks.

flat *noun* **flats**
A **flat** is a set of rooms for living in within a house or larger building.

flat *adjective*
Something smooth and without bumps is **flat**.

flavour *noun* **flavours**
A **flavour** is the taste and smell of something.

flesh *noun* **flesh**
Flesh is the soft substance, including muscle, between the skin and bones of animals.

flight *noun* **flights**
1. A **flight** is a journey made through the air or in space.
2. A **flight** is a set of stairs.
3. A **flight** is an escape.

flipper *noun* **flippers**
1. A **flipper** is a thick wing or limb on a water animal for swimming.
2. **Flippers** are flat rubber devices worn on the feet for swimming.

float *verb* **floats, floating, floated**
1. To **float** means to lie on the top of a liquid.
2. To **float** means to stay in the air, being carried along.

flood *noun* **floods**
A **flood** is a large amount of water overflowing onto normally dry land.

floor *noun* **floors**
1. A **floor** is the part of a building on which people walk.
2. A **floor** is a level or storey of a building.

flow *verb* **flows, flowing, flowed**
To **flow** means to move along smoothly like a stream.

flower *noun* **flowers**
A **flower** is the part of a plant that produces seeds and usually has coloured petals.

flu *noun*
Flu is the short word for influenza. It is an illness where people get a cold and a headache and feel very hot.

fly *noun* **flies**
A **fly** is a small flying insect.

fly *verb* **flies, flying, flew, flown**
To **fly** means to move along in the air.

foal *noun* **foals**
A **foal** is a young horse.

fog *noun*
Fog is a thick mist that is difficult to see through.

fold *verb* **folds, folding, folded**
To **fold** means to bend part of something over another part.

follow *verb* **follows, following, followed**
To **follow** means to go after someone or something.

food *noun* **foods**
Food is something that a person, animal or plant takes in or eats to stay alive.

fool *noun* **fools**
A **fool** is someone who is very silly.

foolish *adjective*
Someone who is very silly is **foolish**.

foot *noun* **feet**
1. A **foot** is the part of the body at the end of the leg.
2. A **foot** is a measure of length, about 30 centimetres.

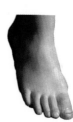

Dictionary fun

Which word describes **poppies** and **tulips**?

? ? ? ?

footprint *noun* **footprints**
A **footprint** is the mark left by a foot or shoe on the ground.

footstep *noun* **footsteps**
A **footstep** is the sound of someone walking.

force *noun* **forces**
1. **Force** is strength or violence.
2. A **force** is a group of people, such as the police or soldiers.

force *verb* **forces, forcing, forced**
To **force** means to use strength to do something.

forecast *noun* **forecasts**
A forecast is saying what is likely to happen.

forehead *noun* **foreheads**
A **forehead** is the part of the face above the eyebrows.

foreign *adjective*
Something or someone who belongs to another country is **foreign**.

foreigner *noun* **foreigners**
A **foreigner** is a person from another country.

forest *noun* **forests**
A **forest** is a large piece of land thickly covered with trees.

forever *adverb*
When something will always be done, it will be done **forever**.

forget *verb* **forgets, forgetting, forgot, forgotten**
To **forget** means to be unable to remember something.

forgive *verb* **forgives, forgiving, forgave, forgiven**
To **forgive** means to stop being angry or annoyed with someone.

fork *noun* **forks**
A **fork** is a tool with three or four points or prongs used for eating and digging.

fort *noun* **forts**
A **fort** is a strong building used by soldiers to protect a place.

fortune *noun* **fortunes**
1. A **fortune** is a lot of money.
2. A **fortune** is a person's luck.

forward *adjective and adverb*
Someone who moves towards the front moves **forward**.

fossil *noun* **fossils**
A **fossil** is the remains of a prehistoric plant or animal that has hardened like rock.

fountain *noun* **fountains**
A **fountain** is a jet of water that shoots up into the air.

fowl *noun* **fowls**
A **fowl** is a bird, such as a hen or cock, that is kept for its meat or eggs.

fox *noun* **foxes**
A **fox** is a wild animal with a long, bushy tail called a brush.

fraction *noun* **fractions**
1. A **fraction** is part of a whole number.
2. A **fraction** is a small part of something.

fragment *noun* **fragments**
A **fragment** is a very small piece of something that is larger.

frame *noun* **frames**
A **frame** is the solid edge round a picture.

free *adjective*
1. Something that does not cost anything is **free**.
2. Someone who can do what he or she wants to do is **free** to do it.

freedom *noun*
Freedom is being able to do what you want to do.

Dictionary fun
Which words are compound words (can be split into smaller words)?

? ? ? ?

a b c d e f g h i j k l m n o p q r s t u v w x y z

freezer *noun* **freezers**
A **freezer** is a kind of refrigerator in which food can be kept for a long time at a very low temperature.

fresh *adjective*
1. Something that is new or newly made is **fresh**.
2. Food that is not canned or frozen is **fresh**.
3. Something that is cool and clean is **fresh**.

fridge *noun* **fridges**
A **fridge** is short for refrigerator (see **refrigerator**).

friend *noun* **friends**
A **friend** is someone you like and want to spend time with.

friendly *adjective and adverb*
Someone who is kind and helpful is **friendly**.

fright *noun* **frights**
A **fright** is a sudden, unexpected fear.

frighten *verb* **frightens, frightening, frightened**
To **frighten** means to make someone afraid suddenly.

frog *noun* **frogs**
A **frog** is a small animal that lives in water and on land.

front *noun* **fronts**
A **front** is the side of something that faces forwards.

frost *noun* **frosts**
Frost is a white ice-like powder that covers things when the weather is freezing.

frown *noun* **frowns**
A **frown** is a wrinkled forehead made when someone is cross or worried.

frozen *adjective*
Something that feels very cold or icy is **frozen**.

fruit *noun* **fruits**
A **fruit** is the part of the plant that holds the seeds. Fruit is often eaten.

fry *verb* **fries, frying, fried**
To **fry** means to cook in hot fat or oil.

fuel *noun* **fuels**
A **fuel** is something that is burned to make heat, for example coal, oil and gas.

full *adjective*
Something that is holding or containing as much as it can is **full**.

fun *noun*
Fun is anything that someone really enjoys doing.

funny *adjective*
1. Something that is amusing is **funny**.
2. Something that is strange is **funny**.

fur *noun* **furs**
Fur is the soft hair that covers the skin of some animals.

furniture *noun*
Furniture is the objects found in a house, for example tables, chairs and beds.

further *adjective and adverb*
Something that is at a greater distance than something else is **further**.

fury *noun* **furies**
Fury is violent anger.

future *noun*
The **future** is the time still to come.

Dictionary fun
Which word is opposite to the past?

? ? ? ?

Gg

gain *verb* **gains, gaining, gained**
To **gain** means to get something that someone did not have before.

galaxy *noun* **galaxies**
A **galaxy** is a very large group of stars.

gale *noun* **gales**
A **gale** is a very strong wind.

galleon *noun* **galleons**
A **galleon** is a Spanish sailing ship used a long time ago.

gallery *noun* **galleries**
1. A **gallery** is a room or building for showing paintings and sculptures.
2. A **gallery** is the upstairs seats in a church or theatre.

galley *noun* **galleys**
1. A **galley** is the kitchen on a ship.
2. A **galley** is a flat sailing boat usually rowed by many slaves or criminals long ago.

gallop *verb* **gallops, galloping, galloped**
To **gallop** means to run like a horse that is moving very quickly.

game *noun* **games**
A **game** is a sport or something that is played with rules.

gang *noun* **gangs**
A **gang** is a group of people who go around and do things together.

gap *noun* **gaps**
A **gap** is an empty space between two things or some free time between two activities.

garage *noun* **garages**
1. A **garage** is a building where vehicles are kept.
2. A **garage** is a place where vehicles are repaired and fuel is sold.

garden *noun* **gardens**
A **garden** is a piece of land where flowers, shrubs, fruit and vegetables are grown.

garlic *noun*
Garlic is a plant like an onion that is used in cooking.

garment *noun* **garments**
A **garment** is a piece of clothing.

gas *noun* **gases**
1. **Gas** is something like air. In some cases it has a strong smell.
2. **Gas** is vapour that is burnt for fuel.

gate *noun* **gates**
A **gate** is a kind of door across an opening in a wall, fence or hedge.

gather *verb* **gathers, gathering, gathered**
To **gather** means to collect or bring together.

general *noun* **generals**
A **general** is a senior officer in the army.

general *adjective*
Something that belongs to most people or things is **general**.

generous *adjective*
Someone who is always willing to share is **generous**.

gentle *adjective*
Someone who is kind and quiet is **gentle**.

gentleman *noun* **gentlemen**
A **gentleman** is a formal word for a man.

geography *noun*
Geography is the study of the Earth, its climate and how people live on it.

gerbil *noun* **gerbils**
A **gerbil** is a small, brown animal with long back legs. They are sometimes kept as pets.

germ *noun* **germs**
A **germ** is a tiny living thing that sometimes makes people ill.

Dictionary fun

Which words (on this page) have a single vowel?

? ? ? ?

get *verb* **gets, getting, got**
1. To **get** means to be given, to buy, to win or to fetch something.
2. To **get** means to become.

ghost *noun* **ghosts**
Some people believe a **ghost** is the spirit of a dead person and can be seen.

giant *noun* **giants**
A **giant** is a huge person from old stories, such as fairy tales.

gift *noun* **gifts**
A **gift** is a present.

gigantic *adjective*
Something that is huge is **gigantic**.

giraffe *noun* **giraffes**
A **giraffe** is a large, African animal with a very long neck.

girl *noun* **girls**
A **girl** is a female child.

give *verb* **gives, giving, gave, given**
To **give** means to let someone have something.

glacier *noun* **glaciers**
A **glacier** is a mass of ice that flows very slowly like a river.

glad *adjective*
Someone who is pleased is **glad**.

glass *noun* **glasses**
1. **Glass** is a hard, clear substance used to make things like windows, mirrors and bowls.
2. A **glass** is a kind of cup without a handle and made of glass.

glasses *noun*
Glasses are a pair of lenses in a frame which people wear to see better.

glide *verb* **glides, gliding, glided**
To **glide** means to move smoothly.

glider *noun* **gliders**
A **glider** is a kind of plane without an engine.

globe *noun* **globes**
A **globe** is a ball with the map of the earth on it.

glove *noun* **gloves**
A **glove** is a covering for the hand and fingers.

gnat *noun* **gnats**
A **gnat** is a small fly that bites.

gnaw *verb* **gnaws, gnawing, gnawed**
To **gnaw** means to keep biting on something.

go *verb* **goes, going, went, gone**
To **go** means to move from one place to another.

go-kart *noun* **go-karts**
A **go-kart** is a small racing car that is often home-made.

goal *noun* **goals**
1. A **goal** is the two posts the ball must pass between to score a point in some games.
2. A **goal** is the point scored in games, such as hockey and netball.

goat *noun* **goats**
A **goat** is a farm animal kept mainly for its milk.

goblin *noun* **goblins**
A **goblin** is a bad or cheeky fairy.

Dictionary fun

Which words (on this page) have a silent **g**?

? ? ? ?

goggles *noun*
Goggles are large glasses worn to protect the eyes.

gold *noun*
Gold is a very valuable, yellow metal.

golf *noun*
Golf is a game played outdoors by hitting a small, white ball with a club into holes.

good *adjective*
1. Something that is enjoyed or well done is **good**.
2. Someone who is well behaved is **good**.
3. Someone who is kind is **good**.

goodbye
Goodbye is something that is said when someone goes away.

goodnight
Goodnight is something that is said when someone goes to bed.

goose *noun* **geese**
A **goose** is a large bird kept for its meat and eggs.

gooseberry *noun* **gooseberries**
A **gooseberry** is a small, green fruit that grows on a prickly bush and can be eaten.

gorilla *noun* **gorillas**
A **gorilla** is a large, African ape.

government *noun* **governments**
A **government** is the group of people who are in charge of a country or state.

grab *verb* **grabs, grabbing, grabbed**
To **grab** means to take something in a forceful, sudden way.

gradual *adjective*
Something that happens slowly happens in a **gradual** way.

grain *noun*
Grain is the seed in a crop, such as corn or wheat.

granary *noun* **granaries**
A **granary** is a building for storing grain.

grand *adjective*
Something that is important or great is **grand**.

grandchild *noun* **grandchildren**
A **grandchild** is a child of a son or daughter.

granddaughter *noun* **granddaughters**
A **granddaughter** is the female child of a son or daughter.

grandparent *noun* **grandparents**
A **grandparent** is the father or mother of a father or mother.

grandson *noun* **grandsons**
A **grandson** is the male child of a son or daughter.

grapefruit *noun* **grapefruits**
A **grapefruit** is a yellow fruit like a large orange.

grape *noun* **grapes**
Grapes are small, soft, green or purple fruits that grow on vines.

grass *noun*
Grass is a plant with narrow, pointed leaves that grows in fields and lawns.

grasshopper *noun* **grasshoppers**
A **grasshopper** is an insect that makes a chirping sound and can jump a long way.

grateful *adjective*
Someone who is very thankful is **grateful**.

gravity *noun*
Gravity is the force that pulls everyone and everything towards the Earth.

Dictionary fun

Which word could come before course, ball and club?

? ? ? ?

gravy *noun*
Gravy is a hot, brown sauce eaten with meat.

graze *verb* **grazes, grazing, grazed**
1. To **graze** means to eat grass that is growing.
2. To **graze** means to scrape the skin on something hard or rough.

grease *noun*
Grease is thick oil or soft, sticky fat.

great *adjective*
1. Something that is very good is **great**.
2. Someone who is very important is **great**.
3. Something that is very large is **great**.

greedy *adjective*
Someone who wants more food or money than is needed is **greedy**.

grew *verb*
This is the past tense of the verb 'to grow' (see **grow**).

grief *noun*
Grief is a very sad feeling.

grip *verb* **grips, gripping, gripped**
To **grip** means to hold something very tightly.

grocer *noun* **grocers**
A **grocer** is a person whose job is to keep a shop selling things, such as tea, sugar, butter and tinned food.

ground *noun* **grounds**
1. **Ground** is the earth or soil.
2. A **ground** is a piece of land used to play on.

group *noun* **groups**
A **group** is a number of people or things that belong together or do things together.

grow *verb* **grows, growing, grew, grown**
1. To **grow** means to get bigger or taller.
2. To **grow** means to plant something in the ground and look after it.

growl *verb* **growls, growling, growled**
To **growl** means to make a rough, angry noise in the throat. Dogs often **growl** when they are angry.

grown-up *noun* **grown-ups**
A **grown-up** is a fully-grown person or adult.

grub *noun* **grubs**
A **grub** is a tiny, wriggling creature that will become an insect.

grunt *verb* **grunts, grunting, grunted**
To **grunt** means to make a sound like a pig.

guard *verb* **guards, guarding, guarded**
To **guard** means to keep someone or something safe or away from other people.

guess *verb* **guesses, guessing, guessed**
To **guess** means to say what you think is right when you do not really know.

guide *noun* **guides**
A **guide** is someone or something that shows people the way to go or how to do something.

guilty *adjective*
Someone who knows he or she has done something wrong feels **guilty**.

guitar *noun* **guitars**
A **guitar** is a musical instrument that has strings across it, which are plucked.

gulf *noun* **gulfs**
A **gulf** is an area of sea in a large bay with a narrow mouth.

gun *noun* **guns**
A **gun** is a weapon that fires bullets from a metal tube.

gunpowder *noun*
Gunpowder is a powder that explodes.

gutter *noun* **gutters**
A **gutter** is a channel at the side of a road or a hollow on the edge of a roof to take rain water away.

Dictionary fun
Which word has three syllables?

? ? ? ?

Hh

habit *noun* **habits**
A **habit** is something that is done without thinking about it because it has been done so often.

had *verb*
This is the past tense of the verb 'to have' (see **have**).

hair *noun* **hairs**
Hair is the fine, soft covering that grows on the heads and bodies of people and animals.

hairdresser *noun* **hairdressers**
A **hairdresser** is a person whose job is to cut, wash and dry people's hair.

hairy *adjective*
Someone or something that is covered in hair is **hairy**.

half *noun* **halves**
A **half** is one of the two equal parts into which something can be divided.

hall *noun* **halls**
1. A **hall** is a very big room like a school hall.
2. A **hall** is the first room or passage inside the front door of a house.
3. A **hall** is a very large house or building like a palace or a town hall.

ham *noun*
Ham is the meat from a pig's leg.

hammer *noun* **hammers**
A **hammer** is a tool used for hitting nails.

hamster *noun* **hamsters**
A **hamster** is a small animal with smooth, brown fur that is kept as a pet.

hand *noun* **hands**
A **hand** is the part of the body at the end of the arm.

handbag *noun* **handbags**
A **handbag** is a small bag that is usually carried by a woman.

handkerchief *noun* **handkerchiefs**
A **handkerchief** is a square of cloth or tissue used for blowing the nose.

handle *noun* **handles**
A **handle** is the part of something that it is held by.

handle *verb* **handles, handling, handled**
To **handle** means to touch, feel or hold something with the hands.

handlebars *noun*
Handlebars are the bars with handles on each end used for steering bicycles.

hang *verb* **hangs, hanging, hung**
To **hang** means to fix something to a hook.

hang-glider *noun* **hang-gliders**
A **hang-glider** is a large kind of kite from which a person can hang while flying.

happen *verb* **happens, happening, happened**
1. To **happen** means to take place.
2. To **happen** means to do something by chance.

happy *adjective*
Someone who is pleased is **happy**.

harbour *noun* **harbours**
A **harbour** is a place where ships can shelter and unload.

hard *adjective*
1. Something that is solid and not soft is **hard**.
2. Something that is difficult is **hard**.
3. Someone who is cruel is **hard**.

harm *verb* **harms, harming, harmed**
To **harm** means to hurt or damage someone or something.

Dictionary fun

Which word means two quarters?

? **?** ? ?

harness *noun* **harnesses**
A **harness** is the set of straps put on a horse's head and neck to control it.

harsh *adjective*
Someone who is cruel is **harsh**.

harvest *noun* **harvests**
Harvest is the time when farmers gather in the crops of corn or fruit they have grown.

hat *noun* **hats**
A **hat** is a piece of clothing for covering the head.

hate *verb* **hates, hating, hated**
To **hate** means to dislike someone or something very much.

have *verb* **has, having, had**
1. To **have** means to own.
2. To **have** means to contain.
3. To **have** means to suffer or enjoy.

hawk *noun* **hawks**
A **hawk** is a large bird that eats small animals.

hay *noun* **hay**
Hay is dried grass used to feed animals.

head *noun* **heads**
1. A **head** is the part of the body containing the face and brains.
2. A **head** is the person in charge.

health *noun* **health**
Health is how a person feels, whether he or she is well or ill.

heap *noun* **heaps**
A **heap** is a pile of things often looking untidy.

hear *verb* **hears, hearing, heard**
To **hear** means to take in sounds through the ears.

heart *noun* **hearts**
1. A **heart** is the part of the body that pumps the blood round it.
2. A **heart** is a symbol shaped like a heart, such as the red heart shape on playing-cards.

heavy *adjective*
Something that weighs a lot is **heavy**.

hedge *noun* **hedges**
A **hedge** is a row of bushes grown to form a wall.

height *noun* **heights**
1. A **height** is the distance from the bottom of something to the top.
2. A **height** is something that is very high.

helicopter *noun* **helicopters**
A **helicopter** is a kind of plane with large blades that spin round.

helmet *noun* **helmets**
A **helmet** is a strong, hard covering to protect the head.

help *verb* **helps, helping, helped**
To help means to do something that makes another person's work easier.

helpful *adjective*
Someone who does something for someone else is **helpful**.

hem *noun* **hems**
A **hem** is the border on a piece of cloth made by turning the edge under and sewing it down.

hen *noun* **hens**
A **hen** is a female bird, especially a chicken.

herd *noun* **herds**
A **herd** is a number of cattle that stay together.

here *adverb*
Something that is in or at this place is **here**.

Dictionary fun
Which word is opposite to gentle?

? ? ?? ?

a b c d e f g h i j k l m n o p q r s t u v w x y z

hide *verb* **hides, hiding, hid, hidden**
1. To **hide** means to get into a place that is out of sight.
2. To **hide** means to put something in a place where it cannot be seen.

high *adjective*
Something that is a long way up is **high**.

hill *noun* **hills**
A **hill** is an area of raised land.

hinge *noun* **hinges**
A **hinge** is the fastener on which a door or gate swings.

hip *noun* **hips**
A **hip** is the bone that sticks out at the top of a leg.

hippopotamus *noun* **hippopotamuses** or **hippopotami**
A **hippopotamus** is a very large, thick-skinned, African animal that lives near water.

history *noun*
History is the study of things that happened in the past.

hit *verb* **hits, hitting, hit**
1. To **hit** means to knock or hurt.
2. To **hit** means to move something like a ball by hitting it.

hive *noun* **hives**
A **hive** is a kind of box to keep bees in.

hobby *noun* **hobbies**
A **hobby** is something interesting that someone enjoys doing in his or her spare time.

hockey *noun*
Hockey is a game played by two teams using sticks to move a ball or puck.

hold *noun* **holds**
1. A **hold** is the part of a ship below deck where the cargo is kept.
2. A **hold** is a grasp or grip.

hold *verb* **holds, holding, held**
1. To **hold** means to have something in the hands.
2. To **hold** means to have room inside for something.

hole *noun* **holes**
A **hole** is a gap or opening in something.

holiday *noun* **holidays**
A **holiday** is a break from school or work.

hollow *noun* **hollows**
A **hollow** is a hole or empty space.

hollow *adjective*
Something that is not solid but has an empty space inside it is **hollow**.

home *noun* **homes**
A **home** is the place where someone lives.

honest *adjective*
Someone who tells the truth and does not cheat or steal is **honest**.

honey *noun*
Honey is a sweet, sticky, yellow food made by bees.

honeycomb *noun* **honeycombs**
A honeycomb is a framework of wax made by bees for storing their eggs and honey.

hood *noun* **hoods**
A **hood** is a covering for the head and neck sometimes joined to a jacket.

hoof *noun* **hoofs** or **hooves**
A **hoof** is the hard part of a horse's foot.

hook *noun* **hooks**
A **hook** is a bent piece of metal or other material for hanging or catching things on.

hop *verb* **hops, hopping, hopped**
To **hop** means to jump on one leg.

hope *verb* **hopes, hoping, hoped**
To **hope** means to feel that something that is wanted will happen.

horizon *noun* **horizons**
A **horizon** is the line where the sky and the land or sea seem to meet.

horizontal *adjective*
Something that is level like the horizon is **horizontal**.

Dictionary fun
Which word contains four different vowels? Which vowel is missing?

?

horn *noun* **horns**
1. A **horn** is a kind of pointed bone growing on the head of some animals, such as cattle and goats.
2. A **horn** is a musical instrument made of brass that is blown.

horrible *adjective*
Something that is frightening or not at all nice is **horrible**.

horror *noun* **horrors**
A **horror** is a feeling of very great fear.

horse *noun* **horses**
A **horse** is a large animal used for riding and pulling carts.

hospital *noun* **hospitals**
A **hospital** is a building in which people who are ill or hurt are looked after.

hot *adjective*
1. Something that is very warm is **hot**.
2. A taste that has a burning flavour like pepper is **hot**.

hotel *noun* **hotels**
A **hotel** is a building where people can pay to have meals and stay the night.

hour *noun* **hours**
An **hour** is a length of time lasting 60 minutes.

house *noun* **houses**
A **house** is a building where people, usually from one family, live.

hover *verb* **hovers, hovering, hovered**
1. To **hover** means to stay in one place in the air.
2. To **hover** means to hang around with nothing to do.

hovercraft *noun* **hovercrafts**
A **hovercraft** is a large vehicle that travels just above the surface of land or water.

how *adverb*
How means in what way.

however *adverb*
However means in spite of this.

howl *verb* **howls, howling, howled**
To **howl** means to make a long, loud cry.

hug *verb* **hugs, hugging, hugged**
To **hug** means to hold someone in your arms in a loving way.

huge *adjective*
Something that is very big is **huge**.

human being *noun* **human beings**
A **human being** is a person.

hump *noun* **humps**
1. A **hump** is a round lump.
2. A **hump** is the round lump on a camel's back.

hung *verb*
This is the past tense of the verb 'to hang' (see **hang**).

hungry *adjective*
Someone who feels the need to eat some food is **hungry**.

hunt *verb* **hunts, hunting, hunted**
1. To **hunt** means to chase after wild animals and try to kill them.
2. To **hunt** means to look for something very carefully.

hurricane *noun* **hurricanes**
A **hurricane** is a storm with a very strong wind.

hurry *verb* **hurries, hurrying, hurried**
To **hurry** means to do something quickly.

hurt *verb* **hurts, hurting, hurt**
To **hurt** means to do something to someone that causes pain or unhappiness.

husband *noun* **husbands**
A **husband** is a man who is married to a woman.

hut *noun* **huts**
A **hut** is a small, simple house or shelter.

hyena *noun* **hyenas**
A **hyena** is an animal like a wild dog whose cry is like a laugh.

Dictionary fun

Can you turn the adjective **huge** into an adverb? Put it into a sentence.

? ? ? ?

Ii

I *pronoun*
I is a word used when referring to yourself.

ice *noun*
Ice is frozen water.

ice *verb* **ices, icing, iced**
To **ice** means to put sugar icing on a cake.

ice cream *noun* **ice creams**
An **ice cream** is a sweet, creamy, frozen food.

iceberg *noun* **icebergs**
An **iceberg** is a very large lump of ice floating in the sea.

icicle *noun* **icicles**
An **icicle** is a thin, pointed piece of ice hanging down from something.

idea *noun* **ideas**
An **idea** is a thought or plan someone has had.

idle *adjective*
Someone who has nothing to do is **idle**.

ill *adjective*
Someone who is not well or sick is **ill**.

illness *noun* **illnesses**
An **illness** is something that makes people ill, such as a cold or chicken-pox.

imaginary *adjective*
Something that is not real is **imaginary**.

imagine *verb* **imagines, imagining, imagined**
To **imagine** means to make pictures in the mind.

imitate *verb* **imitates, imitating, imitated**
To **imitate** means to copy someone.

immediately *adverb*
Something that happens at once happens **immediately**.

impatient *adjective*
Someone who is restless or not patient is **impatient**.

important *adjective*
1. Something that should be thought about seriously is **important**.
2. Someone who is well known and worth respect is **important**.

impossible *adjective*
Something that is not possible is **impossible**.

improve *verb* **improves, improving, improved**
To **improve** means to get better or to make something better.

indoors *adverb*
Something that is inside a building is **indoors**.

infant *noun* **infants**
An **infant** is a very young child.

information *noun*
Information is the facts that tell someone about something.

inhabitant *noun* **inhabitants**
An **inhabitant** is someone who lives in a certain place.

injure *verb* **injures, injuring, injured**
To **injure** means to hurt or damage.

ink *noun* **inks**
Ink is a black or coloured liquid used in pens for writing.

inn *noun* **inns**
An **inn** is a small hotel.

Dictionary fun

Which word could you change into the plural of mouse, by adding an **m**?

? ? ?

insect *noun* **insects**
An **insect** is a small animal with six legs, such as an ant, bee or fly.

inside *adverb and preposition*
An object that is in something else is **inside** it. *The shoes were inside the box.*

instead *adverb*
Something that is in place of something else is **instead** of it.

instruction *noun* **instructions**
An **instruction** is the direction that tells someone how to do something.

instrument *noun* **instruments**
1. An **instrument** is an object used to make musical sounds.
2. An **instrument** is a tool used for doing a job.

intelligent *adjective*
Someone who is clever is **intelligent**.

interest *verb* **interests, interesting, interested**
To **interest** means to make someone want to find out more about something.

interfere *verb* **interferes, interfering, interfered**
To **interfere** means to get in the way and stop something being done properly.

international *adjective*
Something that belongs to more than one country is **international**.

interrupt *verb* **interrupts, interrupting, interrupted**
To **interrupt** means to stop someone who is talking or doing something.

interview *verb* **interviews, interviewing, interviewed**
To **interview** someone means to ask someone questions about a particular subject.

into *preposition*
When someone or something goes inside something it goes **into** it. *They went into the shop to shelter from the rain.*

introduce *verb* **introduces, introducing, introduced**
To **introduce** means to make a person known to other people.

invent *verb* **invents, inventing, invented**
To **invent** something means to plan or make something that has not been thought about or made before.

invention *noun* **inventions**
An **invention** is a plan or object that has never existed before.

inventor *noun* **inventors**
An **inventor** is a person who has a brand-new idea or who makes something that has never been made before.

invisible *adjective*
Something that cannot be seen is **invisible**.

invitation *noun* **invitations**
An **invitation** is words that ask someone politely to come somewhere or do something.

invite *verb* **invites, inviting, invited**
To **invite** means to ask someone to come somewhere or do something.

iron *noun* **irons**
1. **Iron** is a grey, heavy metal used to make steel.
2. An **iron** is a flat piece of metal with a handle, which is heated and used to smooth out clothes after washing them.

irregular *adjective*
Something that is not even or regular is **irregular**.

island *noun* **islands**
An **island** is a piece of land with water all round it.

itself *pronoun*
Itself is it and nothing else.

Dictionary fun
Which word describes Ireland, Greenland and Iceland? (Clue: look in an atlas.) **?**?**?**

Jj

jab *verb* **jabs, jabbing, jabbed**
To **jab** means to poke something roughly.

jacket *noun* **jackets**
A **jacket** is a kind of short coat.

jam *noun* **jams**
1. **Jam** is food made from fruit boiled with sugar.
2. A **jam** is a lot of people or cars crowded together so that they can hardly move.

jam *verb* **jams, jamming, jammed**
To **jam** means to become stuck tight.

jar *noun* **jars**
A **jar** is a container, often made of glass.

jaw *noun* **jaws**
A **jaw** is a bone in the lower part of the face that holds the teeth.

jeans *noun*
Jeans are strong, cotton trousers.

jellyfish *noun* **jellyfish**
A **jellyfish** is an animal that lives in the sea and looks like jelly.

jerk *verb* **jerks, jerking, jerked**
To **jerk** means to move suddenly and not smoothly.

jet *noun* **jets**
1. A **jet** is a liquid or gas that comes forcefully out of a small opening.
2. A **jet** is a plane with jet engines.

jewel *noun* **jewels**
A **jewel** is a precious, beautiful stone.

jigsaw *noun* **jigsaws**
A **jigsaw** is a puzzle made of pieces that fit together to form a picture.

job *noun* **jobs**
A **job** is a task or the work that a person does.

join *verb* **joins, joining, joined**
1. To **join** means to put or fix together.
2. To **join** means to become a member of a group or club.

joint *noun* **joints**
1. A **joint** is a point in the body where two bones fit together.
2. A **joint** is a large piece of meat.

joke *noun* **jokes**
A **joke** is something said or done that makes people laugh.

journey *noun* **journeys**
A **journey** is a distance that someone travels.

judge *noun* **judges**
A **judge** is a person who decides the result either in a court of law or in a competition.

judge *verb* **judges, judging, judged**
To **judge** means to decide the result in a court of law, a competition or an argument.

jug *noun* **jugs**
A **jug** is a container for liquids used for pouring the liquid easily.

juggler *noun* **jugglers**
A **juggler** is someone who entertains people by throwing and catching several things at once.

juice *noun* **juices**
Juice is the liquid from fruit and vegetables.

jump *verb* **jumps, jumping, jumped**
To **jump** means to move up quickly from the ground with both legs in the air.

jungle *noun* **jungles**
A **jungle** is a thick forest in a hot, damp country.

junior *adjective*
Someone who is younger is **junior**.

junk *noun* **junks**
Junk is things that are not wanted any more.

just *adjective*
Something that is fair is **just**.

just *adverb*
1. Something that is exactly what is needed is **just** what is needed.
2. When someone only wanted something, **just** that thing was wanted.

Dictionary fun
Which word rhymes with **loose**?

? **?** ? ?

48

Kk

kangaroo *noun* **kangaroos**
A **kangaroo** is an Australian animal that jumps.

keep *verb* **keeps, keeping, kept**
1. To **keep** means to have something for a long time without giving it away.
2. To **keep** means to look after something safely.
3. To **keep** means to make something stay the same.

kennel *noun* **kennels**
A **kennel** is a small hut for a dog to live in.

kettle *noun* **kettles**
A **kettle** is a container for boiling water.

key *noun* **keys**
1. A **key** is a piece of metal that fits a lock and turns it.
2. A **key** is a kind of button or lever that is pressed to work things like pianos and computer keyboards.

kick *verb* **kicks, kicking, kicked**
To **kick** means to hit out with one or both feet.

kill *verb* **kills, killing, killed**
To **kill** means to make someone or something die.

kilt *noun* **kilts**
A **kilt** is a kind of pleated skirt. They were originally worn by men in Scotland.

kind *noun* **kinds**
A **kind** is a sort or type.

kind *adjective*
Someone who is helpful and loving is **kind**.

king *noun* **kings**
A **king** is a man who has been crowned as ruler of a country.

kiss *verb* **kisses, kissing, kissed**
To **kiss** means to touch someone with the lips as a greeting or as a sign of liking that person.

kit *noun* **kits**
1. A **kit** is a set of tools, clothing or things that are needed for something.
2. A **kit** is a set of pieces needed to make something.

kitchen *noun* **kitchens**
A **kitchen** is a room where food is stored, prepared and cooked.

kite *noun* **kites**
A **kite** is a frame covered with a light material and joined to a long piece of string so that it can be flown in the air.

kitten *noun* **kittens**
A **kitten** is a young cat.

kiwi fruit *noun* **kiwi fruits**
A **kiwi fruit** is a green fruit with a brown, furry, thin skin.

knee *noun* **knees**
A **knee** is the joint in the middle of the leg where it bends.

knife *noun* **knives**
A **knife** is a tool with a long, sharp blade for cutting things.

knight *noun* **knights**
1. A **knight** is a man with the title 'Sir'.
2. A **knight** is a man in the Middle Ages who fought on horseback and wore armour.

knob *noun* **knobs**
A **knob** is a round handle.

knock *verb* **knocks, knocking, knocked**
To **knock** means to hit something or bump into it.

knot *noun* **knots**
A **knot** is the twists made when two ends of string, rope or ribbon are joined together.

know *verb* **knows, knowing, knew, known**
1. To **know** means to be sure of something in your mind.
2. To **know** someone means to have met that person before.

koala *noun* **koalas**
A **koala** is a small, furry, Australian animal, like a small bear.

Dictionary fun
Which words (on this page) have a silent **k**?

? **?** ? ?

a b c d e f g h i j k l m n o p q r s t u v w x y z

Ll

label *noun* **labels**
A **label** is a piece of card or paper put on something to show what it is, what it costs, whose it is or where it is going.

laboratory *noun* **laboratories**
A **laboratory** is a room or building where scientific experiments are done.

lace *noun*
Lace is a fine, pretty material with a pattern of holes in it.

lace *noun* **laces**
A **lace** is a thin cord for fastening shoes.

ladder *noun* **ladders**
A **ladder** is two long bars with crosspieces or rungs used for climbing up or down.

ladle *noun* **ladles**
A **ladle** is a very large spoon used for serving soup.

lady *noun* **ladies**
A **lady** is a polite name for a woman.

ladybird *noun* **ladybirds**
A **ladybird** is a small red or yellow insect with black spots, sometimes called a ladybug.

lake *noun* **lakes**
A **lake** is a large area of water with land all around it.

lamb *noun* **lambs**
A **lamb** is a young sheep.

lamp *noun* **lamps**
A **lamp** is something that produces light.

lance *noun* **lances**
A **lance** is a long spear used by knights on horseback.

land *noun*
Land is all the dry parts of the Earth.

land *verb* **lands, landing, landed**
To **land** means to arrive on land, often from a boat or plane.

lane *noun* **lanes**
A **lane** is a narrow road, often in the country.

language *noun* **languages**
Language is the words spoken or written by people.

lap *noun* **laps**
1. A **lap** is the part of the body from the hips to the knees when a person is sitting down.
2. A **lap** is once around a sports-track.

lap *verb* **laps, lapping, lapped**
To **lap** means to drink with the tongue.

large *adjective*
Something that is big is **large**.

last *verb* **lasts, lasting, lasted**
To **last** means to go on for some time.

last *adjective and adverb*
Something that comes after all the others is **last**.

late *adjective and adverb*
1. Someone who comes after the expected time is **late**.
2. Something that happens near the end of the day, season or some other period of time happens **late**.

laugh *verb* **laughs, laughing, laughed**
To **laugh** means to make the sound when happy or amused.

launch *noun* **launches**
A **launch** is a motor boat.

launch *verb* **launches, launching, launched**
To **launch** means to slide a ship into the water or send a spaceship into space.

lava *noun*
Lava is the hot liquid that pours out of a volcano and cools into rock.

law *noun* **laws**
A **law** is a rule that everybody must obey.

lawn *noun* **lawns**
A **lawn** is an area of a garden covered in short grass.

Dictionary fun

Which word (in the plural) can have its letters moved around to make **scale**?

? ? ? ?

lay *verb* **lays, laying, laid**
1. To **lay** means to put something down.
2. To **lay** means to produce an egg.
3. This is the past tense of the verb 'to lie' (see **lie**).

layer *noun* **layers**
A **layer** is something flat that lies on or inside another surface.

lazy *adjective*
Someone who is not willing to work is **lazy**.

lead *noun* **leads**
1. **Lead** is a soft, very heavy metal.
2. A **lead** is a strap fastened to an animal's collar so that it can be controlled.

lead *verb* **leads, leading, led**
1. To **lead** means to go in front of other people to show them the way.
2. To **lead** means to be in charge of a group of people.

leader *noun* **leaders**
A **leader** is someone or something that leads others.

leaf *noun* **leaves**
A **leaf** is usually flat and grows on trees and other plants. **Leaves** are often green but may change colour during the year.

leak *verb* **leaks, leaking, leaked**
To **leak** means to have a crack or hole that liquid or gas is getting through.

lean *verb* **leans, leaning, leaned, leant**
1. To **lean** means to be or put something in a sloping position.
2. To **lean** means to rest against something.

leap *verb* **leaps, leaping, leaped, leapt**
To **leap** means to jump.

learn *verb* **learns, learning, learned or learnt**
To **learn** means to find out about, or how to do, something.

least *noun*
The least is the smallest amount.

least *adjective and adverb*
Something that is less than all the others is **least**.

leather *noun*
Leather is a strong material made from animal skins.

leave *verb* **leaves, leaving, left**
1. To **leave** means to go away from somewhere.

2. To **leave** means to let something stay where it is.

led *verb*
This is the past tense of the verb 'to lead' (see **lead**).

leek *noun* **leeks**
A **leek** is a long, white vegetable with green leaves and an oniony taste.

left *verb*
This is the past tense of the verb 'to leave' (see **leave**).

left *adjective and adverb*
Something that is on the side opposite the right is on the **left** side.

leg *noun* **legs**
1. A **leg** is one of the parts of the body used for standing and walking.
2. A **leg** is one of the supports on a table or other pieces of furniture.

lemon *noun* **lemons**
A **lemon** is a yellow fruit with a sour taste.

lend *verb* **lends, lending, lent**
To **lend** means to let someone have something for a while and then return it.

length *noun* **lengths**
A **length** is how long something is.

lens *noun* **lenses**
A **lens** is a curved piece of glass or plastic used in things like glasses, telescopes and cameras.

leopard *noun* **leopards**
A **leopard** is a spotted, wild animal from the cat family.

less *adjective and adverb*
Something that is not so much is **less**.

lesson *noun* **lessons**
A **lesson** is the time when something is taught.

Dictionary fun

Which two words sound the same, but are spelled differently?

? **?** ? ?

a b c d e f g h i j k l m n o p q r s t u v w x y z

let *verb* **lets, letting, let**
To **let** means to allow something to happen.

letter *noun* **letters**
1. A **letter** is one of the symbols used to write words such as a, b or c.
2. A **letter** is a written message sent to someone, often by mail.

level *adjective*
1. Something that is smooth and flat is **level**.
2. Things that are equal are **level**.

lever *noun* **levers**
A **lever** is a bar that is pulled down to lift up a heavy object or to work a machine.

library *noun* **libraries**
A **library** is a collection of books, kept for people to read or borrow.

lick *verb* **licks, licking, licked**
To **lick** means to touch something with the tongue.

lid *noun* **lids**
A **lid** is a cover for a box or other container.

lie *verb* **lies, lying, lay, lain**
To **lie** means to be in a flat position, such as in bed.

lie *verb* **lies, lying, lied**
To **lie** means to say something that is not true.

life *noun* **lives**
A **life** is the time between birth and death.

lift *noun* **lifts**
1. A **lift** is a machine for taking people and things from one floor to another.
2. A **lift** is a free ride in someone else's car or other vehicle.

lift *verb* **lifts, lifting, lifted**
1. To **lift** means to move something to a higher level.
2. To **lift** means to pick something up.

light *noun* **lights**
A **light** is something that makes things able to be seen.

light *verb* **lights, lighting, lit**
To **light** something means to start it burning.

light *adjective*
1. Something that is not heavy is **light**.
2. Something that is pale is **light**.

lighthouse *noun* **lighthouses**
A **lighthouse** is a tower with a bright, flashing light to warn ships of danger.

lightning *noun*
Lightning is the flashing, bright light in the sky during a thunderstorm.

like *verb* **likes, liking, liked**
To **like** means to be fond of someone or something.

like *preposition*
Something that is nearly the same as something else is **like** it. *Ann looked like her sister.*

line *noun* **lines**
1. A **line** is a long, thin mark.
2. A **line** is a row of people or things.

lion *noun* **lions**
A **lion** is a large, powerful, wild animal from the cat family.

lip *noun* **lips**
1. A **lip** is one of the edges of the mouth.
2. A **lip** is the edge of something that is hollow.

liquid *noun* **liquids**
A **liquid** is anything that can flow like water.

list *noun* **lists**
A **list** is a group of names or things written down one under the other.

listen *verb* **listens, listening, listened**
To **listen** means to pay attention, to hear something.

little *adjective*
Something that is small is **little**.

live *verb* **lives, living, lived**
1. To **live** means to be alive.
2. To **live** means to have a home somewhere.

Dictionary fun
Which word is associated with safety for ships?

? ? ? ?

a b c d e f g h i j k l m n o p q r s t u v w x y z

living room *noun* **living rooms**
A **living room** is a room with comfortable chairs.

lizard *noun* **lizards**
A **lizard** is a creature with a scaly skin and four legs.

loaf *noun* **loaves**
A **loaf** is a portion of baked bread.

lock *noun* **locks**
1. A **lock** is a fastening to keep a door, window or box closed.
2. A **lock** is a piece of hair.
3. A **lock** is a section of a canal, where the water can be raised or lowered.

lock *verb* **locks, locking, locked**
To **lock** means to fasten with a key.

log *noun* **logs**
A **log** is a piece of a tree that has been cut down.

lonely *adjective*
1. Someone who is sad because of being alone is **lonely**.
2. Something or somewhere that is a long way from anywhere else is **lonely**.

long *adjective*
Something that measures a great distance or lasts a great time is **long**.

long *verb* **longs, longing, longed**
To **long** for something means to want it very much.

look *verb* **looks, looking, looked**
1. To **look** means to use the eyes.
2. To **look** means to seem.

loom *noun* **looms**
A **loom** is a machine for weaving cloth.

loose *adjective*
1. Something that is not tight is **loose**.
2. Something that is not fixed to anything is **loose**.

lose *verb* **loses, losing, lost**
1. To **lose** something means to be unable to find it.
2. To **lose** means to be beaten in a game.

lost *verb*
This is the past tense of the verb 'to lose' (see **lose**).

lot *noun* **lots**
A **lot** is a large number or a large amount.

loud *adjective*
Something that is noisy is **loud**.

loudspeaker *noun* **loudspeakers**
A **loudspeaker** is the part of a radio, television or CD-player that produces the sound.

lounge *noun* **lounges**
A **lounge** is a room with comfortable chairs in it.

love *verb* **loves, loving, loved**
To **love** means to like very much.

lovely *adjective*
Something that is pleasing or beautiful is **lovely**.

low *adjective*
Something that is not high is **low**.

loyal *adjective*
Someone who can always be relied on and trusted is **loyal**.

luck *noun* **luck**
Luck is something that happens by chance.

luggage *noun*
Luggage is the suitcases and bags taken by someone when travelling.

lunch *noun* **lunches**
A **lunch** is a meal eaten in the middle of the day.

lung *noun* **lungs**
Lungs are the two inner parts of the body used for breathing.

lynx *noun* **lynxes**
A **lynx** is a spotted, wild animal from the cat family.

Dictionary fun

What letter does the **s** in lose sound like?

? ? ? ?

Mm

machine *noun* **machines**
A **machine** is something with parts that work together using power to do a job.

made *verb*
This is the past tense of the verb 'to make' (see **make**).

magazine *noun* **magazines**
A **magazine** is a thin book with stories and pictures that comes out each week or month.

magic *noun* **magic**
Magic is the power to do amazing things that cannot be explained.

magnet *noun* **magnets**
A **magnet** is a metal bar that can make pieces of iron and steel move towards it.

make *verb* **makes, making, made**
1. To **make** means to produce something out of other things.
2. To **make** means to cause something to happen.

male *noun* **males**
A **male** is a person or animal that can become a father.

mammal *noun* **mammals**
A **mammal** is any animal that can feed its young with its own milk.

man *noun* **men**
A **man** is a fully-grown male.

manage *verb* **manages, managing, managed**
1. To **manage** means to be in charge of something.
2. To **manage** means to be able to do something that is quite difficult.

manager *noun* **managers**
A **manager** is someone who is in charge of a group of people, such as a football team or the workers in a factory.

mane *noun* **manes**
A **mane** is the long hair on the neck of some animals, such as horses or lions.

many *adjective*
When there are large numbers of people or things, there are **many**.

map *noun* **maps**
A **map** is a diagram showing the locations of different places.

maple *noun* **maples**
A **maple** is a kind of tree whose leaf is the symbol of Canada.

marble *noun* **marbles**
1. A **marble** is a small, glass ball used in some games.
2. **Marble** is a kind of smooth stone used for sculptures and building.

march *verb* **marches, marching, marched**
To **march** means to walk very upright with regular steps.

margarine *noun* **margarines**
Margarine is a food used instead of butter.

mark *noun* **marks**
1. A **mark** is a spot or stain that spoils the thing on which it appears.
2. A **mark** is a number or letter put on a piece of work to show how well it has been done.

market *noun* **markets**
A **market** is a place, usually in the open air, where different things are sold from stalls.

marmalade *noun*
Marmalade is a kind of jam made from oranges, lemons or grapefruits.

marriage *noun* **marriages**
A **marriage** is a the ceremony at which a man and a woman are married.

marry *verb* **marries, marrying, married**
To **marry** means to become someone's husband or wife.

marsh *noun* **marshes**
A **marsh** is an area of very wet ground.

marsupial *noun* **marsupials**
A **marsupial** is an animal, such as a kangaroo, with a pouch for carrying its young.

Dictionary fun

In which words does a **g** sound like a **j**?

? **?** ??

marvellous *adjective*
Something that is wonderful is **marvellous**.

mask *noun* **masks**
A **mask** is a covering for the face to protect or disguise it.

mast *noun* **masts**
A **mast** is a tall pole to hold up sails, aerials or flags.

mat *noun* **mats**
1. A **mat** is a small piece of carpet or other floor covering.
2. A **mat** is a piece of material used on a table to prevent damage.

match *noun* **matches**
1. A **match** is a small stick with a head which bursts into flame when rubbed on a rough surface.
2. A **match** is a game played, usually between two sides.

match *verb* **matches, matching, matched**
To **match** means to be the same as, or similar to, something else.

material *noun* **materials**
1. A **material** is any substance that can be used to make things.
2. **Material** is cloth, such as cotton or wool.

mathematics *noun*
Mathematics is the study of numbers, measurement and shapes.

matter *noun* **matters**
1. **Matter** is anything that can be seen and touched.
2. A **matter** is something that needs to be thought about or done.

matter *verb* **matters, mattering, mattered**
To **matter** means to be important.

mattress *noun* **mattresses**
A **mattress** is a large, thick, soft pad for sleeping on.

may *verb* **might**
1. **May** means can.
2. **May** means will or perhaps.

maybe *adverb*
When something may perhaps happen, **maybe** it will happen.

mayor *noun* **mayors**
A **mayor** is in charge of the town council.

me *pronoun*
Me is when you refer to yourself. *He saw me.*

meadow *noun* **meadows**
A **meadow** is a field of grass.

meal *noun* **meals**
A **meal** is the food eaten at breakfast, lunch, dinner, tea or supper.

mean *verb* **means, meaning, meant**
1. To **mean** means to have a certain explanation.
2. To **mean** means to plan or want.

mean *adjective*
Someone who is not kind is **mean**.

meaning *noun* **meanings**
A **meaning** is an explanation of a word or idea.

measles *noun*
Measles is an illness that makes red spots appear on the skin.

measure *noun* **measures**
A **measure** is a unit for measuring, such as metres for length or kilograms for weight.

measure *verb* **measures, measuring, measured**
To **measure** means to find out how big something is.

measurement *noun* **measurements**
A **measurement** is the amount something measures.

meat *noun* **meats**
Meat is animal flesh used as food.

mechanic *noun* **mechanics**
A **mechanic** is a person whose job is to repair machines.

Dictionary fun

Which word can be rearranged to spell **team**?

? ? ? ?

medal *noun* **medals**
A **medal** is a small, shaped piece of metal given to someone for winning a race, being very brave or doing something very well.

medicine *noun* **medicines**
A **medicine** is a liquid or tablet that a sick person takes to get better.

medium *adjective*
Something that is of average or middle size is **medium**.

meet *verb* **meets, meeting, met**
To **meet** means to come together with someone or something.

meeting *noun* **meetings**
A **meeting** is a group of people who have come together for a particular purpose.

melt *verb* **melts, melting, melted**
To **melt** means to change from a solid into a liquid when heated, as ice turns to water.

member *noun* **members**
A **member** is someone who belongs to a group or club.

memory *noun* **memories**
1. **Memory** is being able to remember things.
2. A **memory** is something that is remembered.
3. A **memory** is the part of a computer that stores information.

mend *verb* **mends, mending, mended**
To **mend** means to repair something that is damaged so that it can be used again.

menu *noun* **menus**
1. A **menu** is a list of the food that can be chosen in a restaurant.
2. A **menu** is a list on a computer screen that shows what the program can do.

mercury *noun* **mercury**
Mercury is a silver-coloured, liquid metal.

mermaid *noun* **mermaids**
A **mermaid** is a creature in stories with a woman's body and a fish's tail instead of legs.

mess *noun* **messes**
A **mess** is something that is untidy or dirty.

message *noun* **messages**
A **message** is a piece of information or a request written down and sent from one person to another.

met *verb*
This is the past tense of the verb 'to meet' (see **meet**).

metal *noun* **metals**
A **metal** is a hard substance that melts when very hot, such as gold and copper.

meteor *noun* **meteors**
A **meteor** is a shooting star, a piece of rock from outer space that glows when it falls to Earth.

meter *noun* **meters**
A **meter** is a machine that measures the amount of something that has been used.

microphone *noun* **microphones**
A **microphone** is a machine for picking up sound waves for recording or sending through loudspeakers.

microscope *noun* **microscopes**
A **microscope** is an instrument for making tiny things look bigger.

microwave *noun* **microwaves**
A **microwave** is a kind of oven that cooks food very quickly.

midday *noun*
Midday is 12 o'clock in the day time.

middle *noun* **middles**
A **middle** is the part of something that is the same distance from both ends or edges.

midnight *noun*
Midnight is 12 o'clock in the night time.

might *verb*
This is the past tense of the verb 'may' (see **may**).

Dictionary fun

Who is the subject of a Hans Christian Andersen story?

? **?** ? ?

a b c d e f g h i j k l **m** n o p q r s t u v w x y z

mild *adjective*
1. Someone who is gentle is **mild**.
2. A food that is not strong is **mild**.

mile *noun* **miles**
A **mile** is a measure of length.

milk *noun*
Milk is a white liquid that female mammals feed their babies.

mill *noun* **mills**
1. A **mill** is a building where corn, rice or wheat are ground into flour.
2. A **mill** is a kind of factory.

millennium *noun* **millenniums** or **millennia**
A **millennium** is a period of 1000 years.

million *noun* **millions**
A **million** is the number 1 000 000.

mind *noun* **minds**
A **mind** is the power to think, feel, understand and remember.

mind *verb* **minds, minding, minded**
1. To **mind** means to look after.
2. To **mind** means to dislike or be worried by something.

mine *noun* **mines**
1. A **mine** is a very deep hole dug to get coal, metal or rock out of the ground.
2. A **mine** is a bomb hidden underground or in the sea to blow up things that pass over it.

mine *pronoun*
Something that belongs to me is **mine**.

miner *noun* **miners**
A **miner** is someone whose job is to work down a mine.

mineral *noun* **minerals**
A **mineral** is any natural substance other than plants that is dug from the ground, such as coal or oil.

minimum *adjective*
Something that is the least amount or the smallest extent is the **minimum**.

minister *noun* **ministers**
1. A **minister** is someone who is in charge of a church.
2. A **minister** is someone who is in charge of a government department.

minor *adjective*
Something that is smaller or less important is **minor**.

mint *noun* **mints**
1. **Mint** is a plant with strong-flavoured leaves used in cooking.
2. A **mint** is a sweet food that tastes of mint.
3. A **mint** is a place where coins are made.

minus *preposition*
Something that has less of something is **minus**. *Nine minus two is seven.*

minute *noun* **minutes**
A **minute** is 60 seconds.

minute *adjective*
Something that is tiny is **minute**.

miracle *noun* **miracles**
A **miracle** is something wonderful that happens which was not thought to be possible.

mirror *noun* **mirrors**
A **mirror** is a shiny surface that reflects things very clearly.

mischief *noun*
Mischief is silly or naughty behaviour.

miserable *adjective*
Someone who is very unhappy is **miserable**.

misery *noun* **miseries**
Misery is suffering by feeling very miserable.

miss *verb* **misses, missing, missed**
1. To **miss** means to fail to catch, hit, see, hear or find something.
2. To **miss** means to be sad because someone has gone away.

missile *noun* **missiles**
A **missile** is a weapon that is thrown by a person or sent by a rocket.

Dictionary fun

Which two words sound the same but are spelled differently?

?

mist *noun* **mists**
A **mist** is damp air that is hard to see through.

mistake *noun* **mistakes**
A **mistake** is something that has been thought or done wrongly.

mix *verb* **mixes, mixing, mixed**
To **mix** means to put things together and stir or shake them into one thing.

mixture *noun* **mixtures**
A **mixture** is something made by mixing different things together.

moan *verb* **moans, moaning, moaned**
1. To **moan** means to make a long, soft, low sound to show pain or trouble.
2. To **moan** means to grumble or complain.

model *noun* **models**
1. A **model** is a small copy of something, such as a train.
2, A **model** is someone whose job is to wear new clothes so people can see what they are like.

modern *adjective*
Something that is in use at the present time and is not old is **modern**.

moist *adjective*
Something that is damp is **moist**.

moisture *noun*
Moisture is damp air which settles on surfaces.

mole *noun* **moles**
A **mole** is a small, furry animal that burrows underground.

moment *noun* **moments**
A **moment** is a very small amount of time.

money *noun*
Money is the metal coins and paper notes used when people buy and sell things.

monkey *noun* **monkeys**
A **monkey** is an animal with long arms and a long tail.

monster *noun* **monsters**
A **monster** is a huge, frightening animal in stories.

month *noun* **months**
A **month** is one of the 12 parts into which a year is divided.

Moon *noun*
The **Moon** is a small planet that goes round the Earth and shines at night.

moose *noun* **moose**
A **moose** is a large, North American deer.

more *adjective* and *adverb*
1. When there is a larger number or amount of things, there is **more**.
2. Something that happens again happens once **more**.

morning *noun* **mornings**
Morning is the early part of the day before midday.

mortar *noun*
Mortar is a mixture of sand, cement and water used to stick bricks together in buildings.

mosque *noun* **mosques**
A **mosque** is a building where people worship.

mosquito *noun* **mosquitoes**
A **mosquito** is an insect that bites.

moss *noun* **mosses**
Moss is a plant that grows in damp places.

most *adjective*
1. Something that happens more than any other happens **most**.
2. Someone who is very helpful is **most** helpful.

Dictionary fun

Which word describes May, July and October?

? ? **!** ? ?

moth noun **moths**
A **moth** is an insect that usually flies at night.

mother noun **mothers**
A **mother** is a female parent.

motorbike or **motorcycle** noun **motorbikes** or **motorcycles**
A **motorbike** or **motorcycle** is a two-wheeled vehicle with an engine.

mountain noun **mountains**
A **mountain** is a very high hill.

mouse noun **mice**
A **mouse** is a small animal with a long tail.

moustache noun **moustaches**
A **moustache** is hair that grows on a man's upper lip.

mouth noun **mouths**
A **mouth** is the part of the face that opens to speak and eat.

move verb **moves, moving, moved**
To **move** means to go or take something from one place to another.

movie noun **movies**
A **movie** is a film.

much adjective
When there is a large amount of something, there is **much**.

mud noun
Mud is wet soil.

muddle verb **muddles, muddling, muddled**
To **muddle** means to mix things up and get them in a mess.

mug noun **mugs**
A **mug** is a kind of cup.

multiply verb **multiplies, multiplying, multiplied**
To **multiply** means to make something a number of times bigger.

mumps noun
Mumps is an illness that makes the sides of the face and neck swell.

murder verb **murders, murdering, murdered**
To **murder** means to kill someone deliberately.

murmur verb **murmurs, murmuring, murmured**
To **murmur** means to speak in a very quiet voice.

muscle noun **muscles**
A **muscle** is one of the parts inside the body, which is used to produce movement.

museum noun **museums**
A **museum** is a place where interesting objects are kept for people to go and see.

mushroom noun **mushrooms**
A **mushroom** is a fungus that can be eaten.

music noun
Music is pleasing sounds made by singing or playing a musical instrument.

must verb
Must means have to.

mustard noun
Mustard is a yellow powder or paste made from mustard seeds. It is used for adding a strong flavour to food.

my pronoun
A book that belongs to me is **my** book.

myself pronoun
Something that I and only I do, I do **myself**.

mystery noun **mysteries**
A **mystery** is something that happens but cannot be explained.

Dictionary fun

Which word describes Everest, K2 and Kilimanjaro? (Clue: look in an atlas.)

? ? ? ?

Nn

nail *noun* nails
1. A **nail** is the hard part that covers the tip of each finger and toe.
2. A **nail** is a short, metal spike used to fasten pieces of wood together.

name *noun* names
A **name** is what someone or something is called.

narrow *adjective*
Something that is thin, not wide, is **narrow**.

nasty *adjective*
1. Something that is unpleasant is **nasty**.
2. Someone who is unkind is **nasty**.

nation *noun* nations
A **nation** is a country and the people who live there.

nationality *noun* nationalities
A **nationality** is being a member of a particular nation.

native *noun* natives
A **native** is a person born in the place being discussed.

natural *adjective*
1. Something that is made by nature and not by people is **natural**.
2. Something that is normal is **natural**.

nature *noun* natures
1. **Nature** is everything in the universe not made by people. It includes plants, animals, rock and stars.
2. **Nature** is the make-up or character of a person or animal.

naughty *adjective*
Someone who behaves badly is **naughty**.

navigate *verb* navigates, navigating, navigated
To **navigate** means to make a form of transport, such as a ship or aircraft, go in the right direction.

navy *noun* navies
A **navy** is a group of ships and the people who sail in them for a country.

near *preposition*
Something that is not far away is **near**. *The dog stayed near his master.*

neat *adjective*
Something that is tidy is **neat**.

necessary *adjective*
Something that is really needed is **necessary**.

neck *noun* necks
A **neck** is the part of the body that joins the head to the shoulders.

necklace *noun* necklaces
A **necklace** is a chain of beads, jewels, gold or silver worn round the neck.

need *verb* needs, needing, needed
1. To **need** means to be without something that is necessary.
2. To **need** means to have to do something.

needle *noun* needles
A **needle** is a thin, pointed instrument used for stitching or knitting.

negative *noun* negatives
1. A **negative** is the word 'no' or 'not'.
2. A **negative** is a film from which photographs are printed.

neighbour *noun* neighbours
A **neighbour** is someone who lives next to or near someone else.

neither *adjective*
Neither means not either.

Dictionary fun

Which word is a compound word (can be split into smaller words)?

? ? ? ?

a b c d e f g h i j k l m n o p q r s t u v w x y z

nephew *noun* **nephews**
A **nephew** is the son of a brother or sister.

nervous *adjective*
Someone who is easily frightened or afraid is **nervous**.

nest *noun* **nests**
A **nest** is a place made by birds and some animals for their babies.

net *noun* **nets**
A **net** is strings or threads knotted to form a web or fabric.

never *adverb*
Something that does not happen or will not happen, happens **never**.

new *adjective*
Something that has just been bought or made or discovered is **new**.

news *noun*
News is information about things that have just happened.

newspaper *noun* **newspapers**
A **newspaper** is large sheets of paper folded together, printed each day or week with the news of politics, business, sports and entertainment.

next *adjective*
1. Something that is nearest to something else is the **next** one.
2. Something that happens straight after something else is the **next** thing.

nib *noun* **nibs**
A **nib** is the pointed part of a fountain pen.

nibble *verb* **nibbles, nibbling, nibbled**
To **nibble** means to eat by taking tiny bites.

nice *adjective*
Something that is pleasant is **nice**.

nickname *noun* **nicknames**
A **nickname** is a name used instead of someone's real name.

niece *noun* **nieces**
A **niece** is the daughter of a brother or sister.

night *noun* **nights**
Night is the time when it is dark, between sunset and sunrise.

nightingale *noun* **nightingales**
A **nightingale** is a bird that sings at night.

nightmare *noun* **nightmares**
A **nightmare** is a very frightening dream.

nimble *adjective*
Someone who moves quickly and easily is **nimble**.

noble *adjective*
Someone who is brave and helpful is **noble**.

nobody *pronoun*
Nobody means no person.

nocturnal *adjective*
Something that is active at night, such as a bird or animal, is **nocturnal**.

nod *verb* **nods, nodding, nodded**
To **nod** means to move the head up and down, showing agreement.

noise *noun* **noises**
A **noise** is a loud sound.

Dictionary fun
Which word rhymes with **white**?

? ? ? ?

none *pronoun*
When there is not any of something, there is **none**.

nonsense *noun*
Nonsense is something that does not mean anything.

noon *noun*
Noon is 12 o'clock in the day time.

no one *pronoun*
No one means no person.

north *noun*
North is the direction in which a compass needle always points.

nose *noun* **noses**
A **nose** is the part of the face used for breathing and smelling.

nostril *noun* **nostrils**
A **nostril** is one of the two openings at the end of the nose.

not *adverb*
Not is a word which changes the meaning of something to its opposite.

note *noun* **notes**
1. A **note** is a short letter or message.
2. A **note** is a single sound in music.

nothing *noun*
Nothing is not anything.

notice *noun* **notices**
A **notice** is something written and put up somewhere for people to read.

notice *verb* **notices, noticing, noticed**
To **notice** means to see something.

nought *noun* **noughts**
Nought is the sign '0' meaning nothing.

novel *noun* **novels**
A **novel** is a long, invented story filling a book.

now *adverb*
When something happens at this moment, it happens **now**.

nowhere *adverb*
When something is not anywhere, it is **nowhere**.

nuisance *noun* **nuisances**
A **nuisance** is someone or something that causes trouble.

number *noun* **numbers**
A **number** is a word or figure showing 'how many', such as 1, 2 or 3.

nun *noun* **nuns**
A **nun** is a woman who is a member of a religious group who live together.

nurse *noun* **nurses**
A **nurse** is someone whose job is to look after people who are ill or hurt.

nursery *noun* **nurseries**
A **nursery** is a room or building where babies or young children play and are looked after.

nut *noun* **nuts**
1. A **nut** is a kind of fruit with a hard shell.
2. A **nut** is a piece of metal that is screwed onto a bolt.

nylon *noun*
Nylon is a very strong material used for making clothes and many other things, such as rope.

Dictionary fun

Which letter does the **y** in nylon sound like?

? **?** ? ?

Oo

oak *noun* **oaks**
An **oak** is a large tree whose seeds are called acorns.

oar *noun* **oars**
An **oar** is a pole with a flat blade at the end used to row a boat.

oasis *noun* **oases**
An **oasis** is a place in a desert with water and plants.

obey *verb* **obeys, obeying, obeyed**
To **obey** means to do what you are told to do.

object *noun* **objects**
An **object** is something that can be seen or touched.

object *verb* **objects, objecting, objected**
To **object** means to say that you do not agree with something.

ocean *noun* **oceans**
An **ocean** is a very large area of salt water.

o'clock *adverb*
O'clock means by the clock. The o' stands for 'of the'.

octopus *noun* **octopuses**
An **octopus** is a creature with eight arms that lives in the sea.

odd *adjective*
1. Something that is strange is **odd**.
2. Things that are not exactly alike are **odd**.
3. Numbers that are not even are **odd**.
4. Something that is part of a pair but is without the other part is **odd**.

offer *verb* **offers, offering, offered**
1. To **offer** means to say that someone can take something if it is wanted.
2. To **offer** means to say that you are willing to do something.

office *noun* **offices**
An **office** is a room where someone or a group of people work.

officer *noun* **officers**
An **officer** is someone in the army, navy or air force who is in charge of others.

often *adverb*
When something happens many times, it happens **often**.

oil *noun* **oils**
Oil is a thick liquid used in heating, in machines and in cooking.

old *adjective*
Someone who has lived a long time or something that was made a long time ago is **old**.

olive *noun* **olives**
An **olive** is the bitter fruit from an olive tree. It can be made into olive oil.

once *adverb*
Something that happened one time or at some time happened **once**.

onion *noun* **onions**
An **onion** is a round vegetable with a strong taste.

open *verb* **opens, opening, opened**
To **open** means to unfasten or make something open.

open *adjective*
Something that is not closed is **open**.

opening *noun* **openings**
An **opening** is a beginning or a space.

opera *noun* **operas**
An **opera** is a kind of play in which most of the words are sung.

opposite *noun* **opposites**
An **opposite** is something that is entirely different from something else.

opposite *adjective*
Someone who is facing something is **opposite** it.

orange *noun* **oranges**
An **orange** is a round, juicy fruit with a thick peel.

orangutan *noun* **orangutans**
An **orangutan** is a large, long-haired ape.

orbit *noun* **orbits**
An **orbit** is the path in space of a planet or satellite moving around another planet.

Dictionary fun

Which word describes the Pacific and the Atlantic? (Clue: look in an atlas.)

? **?** ? ?

a b c d e f g h i j k l m n o p q r s t u v w x y z

orchard *noun* **orchards**
An **orchard** is an area where fruit trees grow.

orchestra *noun* **orchestras**
An **orchestra** is a large group of people playing different musical instruments together.

order *verb* **orders, ordering, ordered**
1. To **order** means to tell someone to do something.
2. To **order** means to ask someone to bring something.

ordinary *adjective*
Something that is usual and not special in any way is **ordinary**.

organ *noun* **organs**
An **organ** is a large musical instrument similar to a piano but with many pedals and the sound comes out through pipes.

organisation (organization) *noun* **organisations (organizations)**
An **organisation** is a group of people who work together.

organise (organize) *verb* **organises, organising, organised**
1. To **organise** means to plan and arrange an event.
2. To **organise** means to get people working together well.

ornament *noun* **ornaments**
An **ornament** is an object used to make a place look more attractive.

ostrich *noun* **ostriches**
An **ostrich** is a very large bird that cannot fly but can run very quickly.

other *adjective and pronoun*
Something that is not the same as the one being discussed is the **other** one.

otter *noun* **otters**
An **otter** is an animal that lives near rivers and eats fish.

ought *verb*
Ought means should.

ourselves *pronoun*
When we do something alone, we do it **ourselves**.

out *adverb*
Something or someone who is not in is **out**.

outside *noun* **outsides**
The **outside** is the outer part of something furthest from the middle.

outside *adverb*
Something that is on the outer side or outdoors is **outside**.

oval *adjective*
Something that is shaped like an egg is **oval**.

oven *noun* **ovens**
An **oven** is the part of a cooking stove in which food is baked or roasted.

over *adverb*
1. When something remains and is not needed, it is **over**.
2. When something has ended, it is **over**.

over *preposition*
1. Something that is above or covering an object is **over** it. *The bird flew over the tree tops.*
2. When there are more than a certain number of things, there are **over** that number. *There were over 100 guests.*

overboard *adverb*
Someone who goes over the side of a boat into the water goes **overboard**.

owe *verb* **owes, owing, owed**
To **owe** means to have to pay money to someone.

owl *noun* **owls**
An **owl** is a bird that flies at night and eats small animals.

own *verb* **owns, owning, owned**
To **own** means to possess something.

oxygen *noun*
Oxygen is one of the gases in the air which animals and plants need to stay alive.

oyster *noun* **oysters**
An **oyster** is a kind of shellfish.

Dictionary fun
What two sounds does the **ch** make in orchard and in orchestra?

? ? ? ?

a b c d e f g h i j k l m n o p q r s t u v w x y z

Pp

pack *noun* **packs**
1. A **pack** is a group of things that belong together, such as a pack of cards.
2. A **pack** is a group of animals, such as wolves, that live and hunt together.

pack *verb* **packs, packing, packed**
To **pack** means to put things in containers, such as bags, suitcases or boxes.

pad *noun* **pads**
1. A **pad** is a set of sheets of writing paper held together along one edge.
2. A **pad** is a soft, thick piece of material.

pad *verb* **pads, padding, padded**
To **pad** means to walk softly.

page *noun* **pages**
A **page** is one side of a piece of paper in a book.

pain *noun* **pains**
A **pain** is an unpleasant feeling in part of the body because of illness or injury.

paint *noun* **paints**
Paint is a liquid that is put on paper or an object to colour it.

paint *verb* **paints, painting, painted**
1. To **paint** means to cover with paint.
2. To **paint** means to make a picture or design with paints.

painting *noun* **paintings**
A **painting** is a picture that has been painted.

pair *noun* **pairs**
A **pair** is two of the same kind of thing.

palace *noun* **palaces**
A **palace** is a very large house in which a king, queen or other important person lives.

pale *adjective*
Something that is a very light colour is **pale**.

palm *noun* **palms**
1. A **palm** is the inside part of the hand between the wrist and the fingers.
2. A **palm** is a tree with large leaves but no branches.

panda *noun* **pandas**
A **panda** is a large, Chinese animal that looks like a black and white bear.

panic *noun*
A **panic** is a sudden fear that cannot be stopped.

pant *verb* **pants, panting, panted**
To **pant** means to take short, quick breaths.

panther *noun* **panthers**
A **panther** is a leopard, usually with black fur.

paper *noun* **papers**
Paper is thin sheets of a substance that can be written and drawn on.

parachute *noun* **parachutes**
A **parachute** is a large piece of cloth that opens like an umbrella and is used to allow someone to drop safely from a plane.

parade *noun* **parades**
A **parade** is a group of people marching or walking along while others watch.

paragraph *noun* **paragraphs**
A **paragraph** is a group of sentences about one topic.

parallel *adjective*
Things such as lines that are always the same distance apart are **parallel**.

parcel *noun* **parcels**
A **parcel** is something wrapped up ready to mail or carry.

pardon *verb* **pardons, pardoning, pardoned**
To **pardon** means to forgive.

parent *noun* **parents**
A **parent** is a mother or father.

park *noun* **parks**
A **park** is a large area of ground like a garden that anyone can walk or play in.

park *verb* **parks, parking, parked**
To **park** means to leave a vehicle somewhere for a while.

Dictionary fun

Which word could come before **weight**, **back** and **work**?

? ? ? ?

parliament *noun* **parliaments**
A **parliament** is a group of people who decide the laws for the country.

parrot *noun* **parrots**
A **parrot** is a brightly coloured bird that can learn to speak by copying.

part *noun* **parts**
A **part** is some but not all of something.

partly *adverb*
When part of something is done but not all of it, it is done **partly**.

party *noun* **parties**
A **party** is a group of people who have met to enjoy themselves.

pass *verb* **passes, passing, passed**
1. To **pass** means to hand someone something.
2. To **pass** means to go by something.
3. To **pass** means to be successful in something.

passage *noun* **passages**
A **passage** is a narrow way through something.

passenger *noun* **passengers**
A **passenger** is someone who is travelling in a vehicle, boat or plane but not in control of it.

passport *noun* **passports**
A **passport** is special papers which must be carried when someone goes to another country.

past *noun*
The **past** is the time that is before now.

past *preposition*
A place beyond somewhere is **past** it. *She ran past some shops to get to school.*

paste *noun* **pastes**
Paste is a wet mixture used to stick things together.

pastry *noun* **pastries**
Pastry is a mixture of flour, fat and water which is rolled out and baked.

pasture *noun* **pastures**
Pasture is land covered in grass where cattle and sheep eat.

pat *verb* **pats, patting, patted**
To **pat** means to touch gently.

patch *noun* **patches**
1. A **patch** is a small piece of material sewn over a hole in a garment.
2. A **patch** is a small piece of ground.

path *noun* **paths**
A **path** is a narrow way to walk along.

patient *noun* **patients**
A **patient** is someone who is being looked after by a doctor or nurse.

patient *adjective*
Someone who can bear pain or trouble without complaining is **patient**.

patrol *noun* **patrols**
A **patrol** is a group of people who are guarding an area.

pattern *noun* **patterns**
1. A **pattern** is a design of lines, shapes and colours.
2. A **pattern** is something that is followed in order to make a copy of something.

paw *noun* **paws**
A **paw** is an animal's foot.

pay *verb* **pays, paying, paid**
To **pay** means to give money for something.

pea *noun* **peas**
A **pea** is a small, round, green vegetable that grows in a pod.

peace *noun*
1. **Peace** is a time when there is no war.
2. **Peace** is a time of quiet, stillness and rest.

Dictionary fun

What is the opposite of war?

? **?** ? ?

peach *noun* **peaches**
A **peach** is a round, juicy, yellow-orange, soft fruit.

peacock *noun* **peacocks**
A **peacock** is a large, male bird with a huge, colourful tail that it can spread out like a fan.

peak *noun* **peaks**
A **peak** is the pointed tip or highest point of something.

peanut *noun* **peanuts**
A **peanut** is like a nut but is a seed that grows underground in a shell.

pear *noun* **pears**
A **pear** is a juicy fruit which is round at the base and narrower at the stalk end.

pearl *noun* **pearls**
A **pearl** is a small, white ball in the shell of some oysters which is used to make jewellery.

pebble *noun* **pebbles**
A **pebble** is a small, round stone.

peck *verb* **pecks, pecking, pecked**
To **peck** means to bite or poke something with the beak.

peculiar *adjective*
Something that is odd or strange is **peculiar**.

pedal *noun* **pedals**
A **pedal** is a part of a machine that is worked by pressing it with the foot.

peel *noun* **peel**
Peel is the skin or rind on some fruit and vegetables.

peep *verb* **peeps, peeping, peeped**
To **peep** means to look at something quickly.

pelican *noun* **pelicans**
A **pelican** is a bird with a very long beak used for catching fish.

pen *noun* **pens**
1. A **pen** is an instrument used for writing with ink.
2. A **pen** is a small fenced-off piece of land for keeping in animals.

pen pal *noun* **pen pals**
A **pen pal** is a friend made by writing letters to each other.

pencil *noun* **pencils**
A **pencil** is an instrument with a very thin stick of lead in it, used for writing and drawing.

pendulum *noun* **pendulums**
A **pendulum** is a rod with a weight on the end which swings from side to side.

penguin *noun* **penguins**
A **penguin** is a black and white seabird. It can swim but cannot fly.

people *noun* **peoples**
People are men, women and children.

pepper *noun* **peppers**
Pepper is a powder made from peppercorns and used to give food a strong, hot taste.

perch *noun* **perches**
A **perch** is something a bird rests on when not flying.

perch *verb* **perches, perching, perched**
To **perch** means to sit on something which might not be very comfortable.

perfect *adjective*
Something that has no faults is **perfect**.

perfectly *adverb*
Something that has been done completely has been done **perfectly**.

performance *noun* **performances**
A **performance** is something done in front of an audience.

Dictionary fun

To which word can you add an **s** to the front to make a small spot?

? ? ? ?

perfume *noun* **perfumes**
A **perfume** is a liquid with a beautiful smell.

perhaps *adverb*
If something will possibly happen, **perhaps** it will happen.

period *noun* **periods**
A **period** is a length of time.

periscope *noun* **periscopes**
A **periscope** is an instrument with mirrors so things out of direct sight can be seen.

permission *noun* **permissions**
Permission is the act of agreeing that something is allowed.

person *noun* **persons**
A **person** is a man, woman or child.

pet *noun* **pets**
A **pet** is an animal kept for company.

petal *noun* **petals**
A **petal** is one of the coloured parts of a flower, often of leaf-like shapes.

pheasant *noun* **pheasants**
A **pheasant** is a brightly-coloured bird, which is sometimes hunted.

phone *noun* **phones**
Phone is short for **telephone**.

photocopier *noun* **photocopiers**
A **photocopier** is a machine for copying writing or drawing.

photo/photograph *noun* **photos/ photographs**
A **photo** is a picture taken with a camera and then printed on paper.

photographer *noun* **photographers**
A **photographer** is someone whose job is to take photos.

piano *noun* **pianos**
A **piano** is a large musical instrument with black and white keys.

pick *verb* **picks, picking, picked**
1. To **pick** means to choose.
2. To **pick** means to gather flowers or fruit from plants or trees.

3. To **pick** means to take or gather something up.

pickle *noun* **pickles**
A **pickle** is a strong-tasting food made from vegetables and vinegar.

picnic *noun* **picnics**
A **picnic** is a meal eaten in the open air.

picture *noun* **pictures**
A **picture** is a drawing, painting or photo.

pie *noun* **pies**
A **pie** is meat or fruit covered in pastry and baked.

piece *noun* **pieces**
A **piece** is a part of something.

pier *noun* **piers**
A **pier** is a long structure built out from the shore and over water for people to walk on.

pig *noun* **pigs**
A **pig** is an animal kept on a farm for its meat.

pigeon *noun* **pigeons**
A **pigeon** is a bird sometimes kept to train to fly home.

pile *noun* **piles**
A **pile** is a number of things heaped one on top of the other.

pill *noun* **pills**
A **pill** is a small tablet.

pillar *noun* **pillars**
A **pillar** is a large post that helps to hold up a building or structure.

pillow *noun* **pillows**
A **pillow** is a cushion for someone's head to rest on in bed.

pilot *noun* **pilots**
1. A **pilot** is the person who flies a plane.
2. A **pilot** is someone who guides a ship in and out of a harbour.

Dictionary fun
Which words begin with an **f** sound?

? ? ? ?

pin *noun* **pins**
A **pin** is a thin piece of metal with a sharp point used to fasten things.

pinch *verb* **pinches, pinching, pinched**
1. To **pinch** means to squeeze painfully.
2. To **pinch** means to steal.

pine *noun* **pines**
A **pine** is an evergreen tree with pine-needles and pine cones.

pine *verb* **pines, pining, pined**
To **pine** means to be very sad and feel ill with longing for someone or something.

pineapple *noun* **pineapples**
A **pineapple** is a large, tropical, yellow fruit.

pipe *noun* **pipes**
1. A **pipe** is a tube for carrying gas or liquid.
2. A **pipe** is a tube with a small bowl at one end used for smoking tobacco.

pirate *noun* **pirates**
A **pirate** is someone who attacks and robs ships at sea.

pistol *noun* **pistols**
A **pistol** is a small gun.

pitch *noun* **pitches**
1. A **pitch** is an area of ground marked out for a game.
2. **Pitch** is a black, thick liquid made from tar.

pitch *verb* **pitches, pitching, pitched**
1. To **pitch** means to put up a tent.
2. To **pitch** means to throw.

pity *noun*
Pity is a feeling of being sorry for someone in pain or trouble.

place *noun* **places**
A **place** is a particular area or location.

place *verb* **places, placing, placed**
To **place** means to put something in a particular spot.

plan *noun* **plans**
1. A **plan** is an arrangement to do something.
2. A **plan** is a map of a building or area of land.

plan *verb* **plans, planning, planned**
To **plan** means to arrange to do something.

planet *noun* **planets**
A planet is a sphere in space that travels around another, such as the Earth around the Sun, or the Moon around Earth.

plank *noun* **planks**
A **plank** is a long, flat piece of wood.

plant *noun* **plants**
A **plant** is any living thing that is not an animal, such as a flower or a tree.

plaster *noun* **plasters**
Plaster is a mixture that is spread over walls and ceilings and sets hard.

plastic *noun* **plastics**
Plastic is a strong substance made from chemicals and used to make all kinds of things.

Plasticine *noun*
Plasticine is a soft substance used in making models.

plate *noun* **plates**
A **plate** is a flat dish.

platform *noun* **platforms**
1. A **platform** is the raised area in a station where people stand waiting for a train.
2. A **platform** is a flat, raised surface, such as a stage.

play *noun* **plays**
A **play** is a story acted on a stage or on television.

play *verb* **plays, playing, played**
1. To **play** means to be in a game or to have fun.
2. To **play** means to make music with an instrument.

player *noun* **players**
A **player** is someone who plays in a game or on a musical instrument.

Dictionary fun

Which word describes Pluto, Mars and Saturn?

? ? ? ?

please *verb* **pleases, pleasing, pleased**
1. To **please** means to make someone happy.
2. **Please** is used when asking for something politely.

pleasure *noun* **pleasures**
Pleasure is the feeling of being pleased or happy.

plenty *noun*
Plenty is as much or more than is needed.

pluck *verb* **plucks, plucking, plucked**
1. To **pluck** means to pull the feathers off a bird.
2. To **pluck** means to pick flowers or fruit.
3. To **pluck** means to play a musical instrument by pulling a string and letting it go quickly.

plug *noun* **plugs**
1. A **plug** is a part on the end of a cord that fits into an electric socket.
2. A **plug** is something used to fill a hole.

plunge *verb* **plunges, plunging, plunged**
To **plunge** means to jump or put something into water suddenly.

plural *noun* **plurals**
A **plural** is the form of a word used to mean there is more than one.

plus *preposition*
When something is added, it is **plus** that thing. *Four plus three is seven.*

pocket *noun* **pockets**
A **pocket** is a small bag or patch sewn on a garment to keep things in.

pod *noun* **pods**
A **pod** is a long case that grows on some plants and contains the seeds.

poem *noun* **poems**
A **poem** is a piece of writing, laid out in lines, that has a rhythm. It sometimes rhymes.

poetry *noun*
Poetry is poems.

point *noun* **points**
1. A **point** is the sharp end of something, such as a pin.
2. A **point** is a mark scored when playing a game.

point *verb* **points, pointing, pointed**
1. To **point** means to show the position of something using a finger.
2. To **point** means to aim a weapon.

poison *noun* **poisons**
A **poison** is a substance which can kill or harm a person, animal or plant.

police *noun*
The **police** are the people whose job is to make sure everyone keeps the law and catch those that do not.

polish *verb* **polishes, polishing, polished**
To **polish** means to rub something to make it shine.

polite *adjective*
Someone who has good manners is **polite**.

pollen *noun*
Pollen is the yellow powder inside a flower.

pond *noun* **ponds**
A **pond** is a small lake.

pony *noun* **ponies**
A **pony** is a small horse.

pool *noun* **pools**
1. A **pool** is a pond or puddle.
2. A **pool** is a large tank of for swimming in.
3. **Pool** is a game played with 16 balls and a stick called a cue.

poor *adjective*
1. Someone who has not got much money is **poor**.
2. Something that is bad is **poor**.

poppy *noun* **poppies**
A **poppy** is a flower that usually has red petals.

Dictionary fun

Which word is the opposite of singular?

? ? ? ?

popular *adjective*
Someone who is liked by a lot of people is **popular**.

population *noun* **populations**
A **population** is the total number of people living in a place.

pork *noun*
Pork is meat from a pig.

porridge *noun*
Porridge is a food made from boiling oats in milk or water.

port *noun* **ports**
A **port** is a harbour where ships come to shore.

porthole *noun* **portholes**
A **porthole** is a small, round window in the side of a ship.

position *noun* **positions**
1. A **position** is the place where something is or should be.
2. A **position** is the way something or someone is arranged.

possible *adjective*
Something that can be done or can happen is **possible**.

post *noun* **posts**
A **post** is a pole fixed in the ground.

post *verb* **posts, posting, posted**
To **post** means to mail a letter, postcard or parcel.

postcard *noun* **postcards**
A **postcard** is a card, often with a picture on one side, on which a message can be written and then sent by post.

post office *noun* **post offices**
A **post office** is a place where stamps are sold and letters and parcels are sorted.

poster *noun* **posters**
A **poster** is a sheet of paper with pictures and writing on it to display on a wall.

pot *noun* **pots**
A **pot** is a round container, such as a a flower pot.

potato *noun* **potatoes**
A **potato** is a vegetable which grows underground.

pottery *noun*
Pottery is pots and other items made from clay which is baked.

pouch *noun* **pouches**
1. A **pouch** is a small bag.
2. A **pouch** is a kind of pocket some animals, such as kangaroos, have in their skin.

pound *noun* **pounds**
A **pound** is a unit of money equal to 100 pence.

pour *verb* **pours, pouring, poured**
To **pour** means to make liquid flow out of something.

powerful *adjective*
Someone who is very strong or important is **powerful**.

practice *noun* **practices**
A **practice** is the time spent doing something that is done many times in order to get better at it.

practise *verb* **practises, practising, practised**
To **practise** means to do something repeatedly in order to get better at it.

prawn *noun* **prawns**
A **prawn** is a shellfish like a large shrimp.

pray *verb* **prays, praying, prayed**
To **pray** means to talk to God or gods.

prayer *noun* **prayers**
A **prayer** is what someone makes when he or she is talking to God or gods.

precious *adjective*
Something that is very valuable or very loved is **precious**.

prefer *verb* **prefers, preferring, preferred**
To **prefer** means to like one thing more than another.

Dictionary fun

Which word can you change to **tough** by altering two letters?

? **?** ??

prehistoric *adjective*
Something that lived or happened a long time ago, before there was writing, is **prehistoric**.

prepare *verb* **prepares, preparing, prepared**
To **prepare** means to get something ready.

present *noun* **presents**
1. A **present** is something given to someone.
2. The **present** is the time now.

present *verb* **presents, presenting, presented**
To **present** means to give someone something.

present *adjective*
Someone who is here is **present**.

preserve *verb* **preserves, preserving, preserved**
To **preserve** means to keep something safe or in good condition.

president *noun* **presidents**
1. A **president** is the head of a country that does not have a king or queen.
2. A **president** is the person in charge of a club or organisation.

press *noun*
The **press** is the newspapers.

press *verb* **presses, pressing, pressed**
1. To **press** means to push hard on something.
2. To **press** means to make something smooth and flat.

pretend *verb* **pretends, pretending, pretended**
To **pretend** means to behave as if something that is not true is true.

pretty *adjective*
Someone or something that is attractive to look at is **pretty**.

prevent *verb* **prevents, preventing, prevented**
To **prevent** means to stop something from happening.

price *noun* **prices**
A **price** is how much money has to be paid for something.

prick *verb* **pricks, pricking, pricked**
To **prick** means to make a small hole in something using a sharp point.

priest *noun* **priests**
A **priest** is a person who leads worship and helps people understand their God.

primary *adjective*
Something that is first in importance or in order is **primary**.

prince *noun* **princes**
A **prince** is the son of a king or queen or a male member of a royal family.

princess *noun* **princesses**
A **princess** is the daughter of a king or queen or a female member of a royal family.

print *verb* **prints, printing, printed**
1. To **print** means to write with letters that are not joined together.
2. To **print** means to put words and pictures on to paper using a machine.

prison *noun* **prisons**
A **prison** is a place where criminals are kept.

private *adjective*
1. Something that is not to be known by other people is **private**.
2. Something that is not shared or used by everyone is **private**.

prize *noun* **prizes**
A **prize** is something given to a winner.

probable *adjective*
Something that is likely to happen or to be true is **probable**.

problem *noun* **problems**
A **problem** is a difficulty to be answered or overcome.

project *noun* **projects**
1. A **project** is the task of finding out about a topic and writing about it.
2. A **project** is a plan.

Dictionary fun

Which word is the opposite of **public**?

? ? ? ?

a b c d e f g h i j k l m n o p q r s t u v w x y z

programme/ program *noun* **programmes/ programs**
1. A **programme** is a show, play or other item on the radio or television.
2. A **programme** is a leaflet giving details of a play or other event.
3. A **program** is a set of instructions for a computer.

promise *verb* **promises, promising, promised**
To **promise** means to say that something will definitely be done or not be done.

prong *noun* **prongs**
A **prong** is one of the spikes on the end of a fork.

properly *adverb*
Something that is done correctly is done **properly**.

proud *adjective*
1. Someone who is very pleased because something has been done well is **proud**.
2. Someone who feels more important than he or she really is, is **proud**.

provide *verb* **provides, providing, provided**
To **provide** means to supply something that is needed.

public *noun*
The **public** is all people.

public *adjective*
Something that is for everyone is **public**.

pudding *noun* **puddings**
A **pudding** is a sweet food eaten after the main course of a meal.

puddle *noun* **puddles**
A **puddle** is a small pool of water made by rain.

pull *verb* **pulls, pulling, pulled**
To **pull** means to get hold of something and try to make it move towards you.

pump *noun* **pumps**
A **pump** is a machine for forcing liquid or air through pipes.

pump *verb* **pumps, pumping, pumped**
To **pump** means to use a pump.

pumpkin *noun* **pumpkins**
A **pumpkin** is a very large, orange fruit.

puncture *noun* **punctures**
A **puncture** is a hole made by a sharp object.

pupil *noun* **pupils**
1. A **pupil** is someone who is learning from a teacher.
2. A **pupil** is the round opening in the middle of the eye that looks black.

puppet *noun* **puppets**
A **puppet** is a kind of doll that can be moved by hands, rods or strings attached to it.

puppy *noun* **puppies**
A **puppy** is a young dog.

pure *adjective*
Something that has nothing else mixed with it is **pure**.

purple *adjective*
Something that is reddish-blue in colour is **purple**.

purse *noun* **purses**
A **purse** is a small bag for keeping money in.

push *verb* **pushes, pushing, pushed**
To **push** means to put the hands on something and move it away from you.

put *verb* **puts, putting, put**
To **put** means to place something in a particular position or place.

puzzle *noun* **puzzles**
A **puzzle** is a problem or game that is difficult to solve.

puzzle *verb* **puzzles, puzzling, puzzled**
To **puzzle** means to think very hard about a problem.

pyjamas *noun*
Pyjamas arethe clothing, usually the top and bottom, worn in bed.

pyramid *noun* **pyramids**
1. A **pyramid** is a solid shape with a flat base and sloping sides that meet in a point.
2. A **pyramid** is a large, stone building in the shape of a pyramid made by the ancient Egyptians for the body of a dead king or queen.

Dictionary fun

In which word does a **u** sound like a **w**?

? **?** ? ?

Qq

quack *verb* **quacks, quacking, quacked**
To **quack** means to make a sound like a duck.

quail *noun* **quails**
A **quail** is a small, flightless bird that can be eaten.

quail *verb* **quails, quailing, quailed**
To **quail** means to look very frightened.

quality *noun* **qualities**
Quality is how good or bad something is.

quantity *noun* **quantities**
A **quantity** is an amount of something.

quarrel *verb* **quarrels, quarrelling, quarrelled**
To **quarrel** means to argue with someone in an angry way.

quarry *noun* **quarries**
A **quarry** is a place where rock is dug out of the ground to use in building.

quarter *noun* **quarters**
A **quarter** is one of the four equal parts into which something can be divided.

quay *noun* **quays**
A **quay** is a place in a harbour where ships are loaded and unloaded.

queen *noun* **queens**
A **queen** is a woman who has been crowned ruler of a country or is a king's wife.

queer *adjective*
Something that is strange is **queer**.

quench *verb* **quenches, quenching, quenched**
1. To **quench** means to end someone's thirst.
2. To **quench** means to put out a fire.

question *noun* **questions**
A **question** is something that is asked when an answer is wanted.

queue *noun* **queues**
A **queue** is a line of people or vehicles waiting for something.

quick *adjective*
1. Something that is moving fast is **quick**.

2. Someone who does something in less time than expected is **quick**.

quickly *adverb*
When something is done speedily, it is done **quickly**.

quiet *adjective*
Someone who does something with very little noise is **quiet**.

quietly *adverb*
When something is done with very little noise it is done **quietly**.

quill *noun* **quills**
A **quill** is a large feather, particularly one used as a pen.

quilt *noun* **quilts**
A **quilt** is a padded cover for a bed.

quite *adverb*
1. When something has been completely done, it is **quite** done.
2. Something that is rather good is **quite** good.

quiver *noun* **quivers**
A **quiver** is a bag for holding arrows.

quiver *verb* **quivers, quivering, quivered**
To **quiver** means to shake or tremble.

quiz *noun* **quizzes**
A **quiz** is a set of questions to see how much someone knows.

Dictionary fun

What word sounds like **quay** and is used to open doors?

? ? ? ?

74

Rr

rabbit *noun* **rabbits**
A **rabbit** is an animal with long ears that lives in a burrow.

race *noun* **races**
A **race** is a competition in which people try to be the first to finish.

rack *noun* **racks**
A **rack** is a set of bars for supporting things.

radar *noun* **radars**
Radar is a radio system that can detect objects in its range.

radio *noun* **radios**
A **radio** is a machine for receiving radio broadcasts or programmes.

raft *noun* **rafts**
A **raft** is a flat, floating platform made from wood or other materials.

rag *noun* **rags**
A **rag** is a torn piece of cloth.

raid *noun* **raids**
A **raid** is a sudden attack.

rail *noun* **rails**
1. A **rail** is a long bar or rod.
2. A **rail** is a long, steel bar forming part of a railway line.

railing *noun* **railings**
A **railing** is a fence made of rails.

railway *noun* **railways**
A **railway** is a set of rails or tracks on which trains run.

rain *noun* **rains**
Rain is drops of water that fall from clouds.

rainbow *noun* **rainbows**
A **rainbow** is a curve of coloured light seen in the sky when the sun shines through rain.

raise *verb* **raises, raising, raised**
1. To **raise** means to lift up something.
2. To **raise** means to collect money, people or things needed for something.

raisin *noun* **raisins**
A **raisin** is a dried grape.

rake *noun* **rakes**
A **rake** is a tool with a row of spikes used to gather leaves and other materials in the garden.

ram *noun* **rams**
A **ram** is a male sheep.

ram *verb* **rams, ramming, rammed**
To **ram** means to push something very hard.

ranch *noun* **ranches**
A **ranch** is a large, North American cattle farm.

range *noun* **ranges**
A **range** is a large farm that raises cattle, sheep or horses.

rapid *adjective*
Someone or something that is very quick is **rapid**.

rapids *noun*
Rapids are part of a river where the water flows speedily over rocks.

rare *adjective*
Something that is uncommon or not often found is **rare**.

raspberry *noun* **raspberries**
A **raspberry** is a small, soft, red fruit.

rat *noun* **rats**
A **rat** is an animal that looks like a large mouse.

rattle *noun* **rattles**
A **rattle** is a baby's toy which makes a noise when shaken.

rattle *verb* **rattles, rattling, rattled**
To **rattle** means to make quick, short sounds when shaking something.

rattlesnake *noun* **rattlesnakes**
A **rattlesnake** is a poisonous, North American snake which makes a rattling noise with its tail.

raw *adjective*
Something that is not cooked is **raw**.

ray *noun* **rays**
A **ray** is a thin beam or line of light.

razor *noun* **razors**
A **razor** is an instrument with a sharp blade used for shaving.

Dictionary fun
Which word could be white or wild?

? ? ? ?

reach *verb* **reaches, reaching, reached**
1. To **reach** means to stretch out the hand towards something.
2. To **reach** means to arrive somewhere.

read *verb* **reads, reading, read**
To **read** means to be able to understand words that are written down.

ready *adjective*
1. Someone who is willing and able to do something straight away is **ready**.
2. Something that is prepared for use is **ready**.

real *adjective*
Something that is not imaginary and not a copy is **real**.

really *adverb*
When something has truly happened, it has **really** happened.

reason *noun* **reasons**
A **reason** is an explanation.

receive *verb* **receives, receiving, received**
To **receive** means to take something that has been given or sent.

recipe *noun* **recipes**
A **recipe** is the instructions for cooking something.

recite *verb* **recites, reciting, recited**
To **recite** means to say something that has been learned by heart.

recognise *verb* **recognises, recognising, recognised**
To **recognise** means to know who someone is because you have seen that person before.

record *noun* **records**
1. A **record** is a disk that makes music when turned on a record-player.
2. A **record** is the best performance of something.

record *verb* **records, recording, recorded**
To **record** means to put sounds or images on tape, disk or some other device.

reed *noun* **reeds**
A **reed** is a grass-like plant that grows in or near water.

reef *noun* **reefs**
A **reef** is a line of rocks or coral at or near the surface of the sea.

reel *noun* **reels**
1. A **reel** is a round object on which things, such as cotton or fishing lines are wound.
2. A **reel** is a Scottish dance.

reel *verb* **reels, reeling, reeled**
To **reel** means to stagger due to dizziness.

reflection *noun* **reflections**
A **reflection** is the picture seen in a mirror, water or shiny surface.

refrigerator *noun* **refrigerators**
A **refrigerator** is an electric container for keeping food cool and fresh.

refuse *verb* **refuses, refusing, refused**
To **refuse** means to say that you will not do something you are told to do, or do not take something that is offered to you.

register *noun* **registers**
A **register** is a book containing a list of names and addresses.

regular *adjective*
1. Something that happens at equal intervals is **regular**.
2. Something that is normal is **regular**.

reign *noun* **reigns**
A **reign** is the time when a certain person is king or queen.

reign *verb* **reigns, reigning, reigned**
To **reign** means to be king or queen.

rein *noun* **reins**
A **rein** is a long strap used to guide a horse.

reindeer *noun* **reindeer**
A **reindeer** is a type of deer that lives in cold countries.

relative *noun* **relatives**
A **relative** is a person who belongs to the same family.

relax *verb* **relaxes, relaxing, relaxed**
To **relax** means to rest by becoming less stiff and tense.

Dictionary fun

Which two words sound the same as **rain**?

? ? **!** ? ?

remain *verb* **remains, remaining, remained**
1. To **remain** means to stay.
2. To **remain** means to be left over.

remember *verb* **remembers, remembering, remembered**
To **remember** means to keep something in the mind and not forget it.

remind *verb* **reminds, reminding, reminded**
To **remind** means to help someone to remember something.

remove *verb* **removes, removing, removed**
To **remove** means to take something away.

rent *noun* **rents**
The **rent** is a payment made weekly or monthly to someone for the use of something.

repair *verb* **repairs, repairing, repaired**
To **repair** means to mend something.

repeat *verb* **repeats, repeating, repeated**
To **repeat** means to do or say something again.

reply *verb* **replies, replying, replied**
To **reply** means to answer.

report *verb* **reports, reporting, reported**
To **report** means to give information about something by writing or saying it.

reporter *noun* **reporters**
A **reporter** is someone who collects news or information for a newspaper, radio or television broadcast.

reptile *noun* **reptiles**
A **reptile** is a cold-blooded animal that has a backbone and lays eggs, such as a snake or tortoise.

rescue *verb* **rescues, rescuing, rescued**
To **rescue** means to save someone or something from danger.

rest *noun* **rests**
1. A **rest** is a break from work or from activity.
2. The **rest** is the part that is left.
3. The **rest** is the other people or things.

rest *verb* **rests, resting, rested**
To **rest** means to have a break from activity and relax by sitting or lying down.

restaurant *noun* **restaurants**
A **restaurant** is a place where meals can be bought and eaten.

result *noun* **results**
1. A **result** is something that happens because other things have happened.
2. A **result** is the final score in a game, competition or test.

retreat *verb* **retreats, retreating, retreated**
To **retreat** means to go back.

return *verb* **returns, returning, returned**
1. To **return** means to come or go back somewhere.
2. To **return** means to give something back.

reward *noun* **rewards**
A **reward** is a prize or present given to someone for doing something well.

rhinoceros *noun* **rhinoceroses**
A **rhinoceros** is a very large animal with one or two horns on its nose.

rhyme *noun* **rhymes**
A **rhyme** is a word that sounds the same at the end as another word, such as cat and mat.

rhythm *noun* **rhythms**
A **rhythm** is the pattern of sounds made in music, poetry or movements.

ribbon *noun* **ribbons**
A **ribbon** is a narrow strip of thin material.

rice *noun*
Rice is a grain which is cooked in liquid.

rich *adjective*
Someone who has a lot of money is **rich**.

riddle *noun* **riddles**
A **riddle** is a question or puzzle which is a kind of joke.

ride *verb* **rides, riding, rode, ridden**
1. To **ride** means to sit on something like a horse or bicycle and control it as it moves.
2. To **ride** means to travel in a vehicle.

Dictionary fun
Which word describes a lizard and a turtle?

? ? ? ?

a b c d e f g h i j k l m n o p q **r** s t u v w x y z

right *noun*
The **right** is the side opposite the left.

right *adjective*
1. Something that is correct is **right**.
2. Something that is fair is **right**.

right *adverb*
Someone who turns round completely turns **right** round.

rim *noun* **rims**
A **rim** is the outer edge of a wheel or other round object.

ring *noun* **rings**
A **ring** is a circle or an object in the shape of a circle.

ring *verb* **rings, ringing, rang, rung**
1. To **ring** means to make a bell sound.
2. To **ring** means to telephone.

rip *verb* **rips, ripping, ripped**
To **rip** means to tear.

ripe *adjective*
Something that is ready to be picked or eaten is **ripe**.

ripple *noun* **ripples**
A **ripple** is a tiny movement or wave on the surface of water.

rise *verb* **rises, rising, rose, risen**
1. To **rise** means to go up.
2. To **rise** means to get up.

river *noun* **rivers**
A **river** is a very large stream of water which flows into the sea or a lake.

road *noun* **roads**
A **road** is a way with a hard surface for vehicles to go along.

roar *verb* **roars, roaring, roared**
To **roar** means to make a very loud, deep sound like a lion.

roast *verb* **roasts, roasting, roasted**
To **roast** means to cook meat or vegetables in the oven or over a fire.

rob *verb* **robs, robbing, robbed**
To **rob** means to steal something.

robbery *noun* **robberies**
A **robbery** is the stealing of things from others.

robin *noun* **robins**
A **robin** is a brown bird with a red breast.

robot *noun* **robots**
A **robot** is a machine that does the work of a person or animal.

rock *noun* **rocks**
1. A **rock** is a very large stone.
2. **Rock** is the solid material that makes up most of the Earth's crust.

rock *verb* **rocks, rocking, rocked**
To **rock** means to move gently backwards and forwards.

rocket *noun* **rockets**
1. A **rocket** is a type of firework.
2. A **rocket** is a metal tube used to launch spacecraft.

rod *noun* **rods**
A **rod** is a long, thin stick or bar.

rodent *noun* **rodents**
A **rodent** is an animal, such as a rat or squirrel, that gnaws things.

roll *noun* **rolls**
1. A **roll** is something curled into a tube shape.
2. A **roll** is a very small loaf of bread.

roll *verb* **rolls, rolling, rolled**
To **roll** means to turn over and over like a wheel moving along the ground.

Rollerblade *noun* **Rollerblades**
A **Rollerblade** is one of a pair of boots with small wheels in a line at the bottom.

roof *noun* **roofs**
A **roof** is the part which covers the top of a building or vehicle.

room *noun* **rooms**
1. A **room** is a space with walls around it inside a building.
2. **Room** is space for someone or something.

root *noun* **roots**
A **root** is the part of a plant that grows underground.

Dictionary fun

Which word describes the Nile, the Colorado and the Amazon? (Clue: look in an atlas.) **?** **?** ? ?

a b c d e f g h i j k l m n o p q r s t u v w x y z

rope *noun* **ropes**
A **rope** is very thick string made from strong threads twisted together.

rose *noun* **roses**
A **rose** is a flower with a beautiful scent and thorns on its stem.

rose *verb*
This is the past tense of the verb 'to rise' (see **rise**).

rough *adjective*
1. Something that is not smooth is **rough**.
2. Someone who is not gentle is **rough**.
3. Something that is not exact is **rough**.

round *adjective*
Something shaped like a circle or ball is **round**.

round *preposition*
Something that is on all sides of something is **round** it. *There is a high fence round the prison.*

roundabout *noun* **roundabouts**
1. A **roundabout** is an amusement at a fair on which people can ride round and round.
2. A **roundabout** is a place where roads meet and vehicles have to go around a circle.

row *noun* **rows**
1. A **row** is a line of people or things.
3. A **row** is a quarrel.

row *verb* **rows, rowing, rowed**
To **row** means to move a boat along using oars.

royal *adjective*
Something belonging to a king or queen is **royal**.

rub *verb* **rubs, rubbing, rubbed**
To **rub** means to move something backwards and forwards on or against another thing.

rubber *noun* **rubbers**
1. **Rubber** is a material that stretches, bends and bounces.
2. A **rubber** is a piece of rubber used for removing pencil marks. It is also called an eraser.

rubbish *noun*
1. **Rubbish** is things that are no longer wanted.
2. **Rubbish** is nonsense.

rude *adjective*
Someone who is not polite is **rude**.

rule *noun* **rules**
A **rule** is a law or something that everyone should obey.

rule *verb* **rules, ruling, ruled**
To **rule** means to be in charge of everyone in a country.

ruler *noun* **rulers**
1. A **ruler** is someone who is in charge of a country.
2. A **ruler** is a strip of wood, plastic or metal with straight edges for measuring and drawing straight lines.

run *verb* **runs, running, ran, run**
To **run** means to move with long, quick strides.

rung *noun* **rungs**
A **rung** is one of the bars used as steps on a ladder.

runner *noun* **runners**
A **runner** is someone who runs, especially in a race.

runway *noun* **runways**
A **runway** is the surface used by aircraft when taking off or landing.

rush *verb* **rushes, rushing, rushed**
To **rush** means to move very quickly.

rust *noun*
Rust is the rough, reddish-brown substance that forms on iron after it gets wet.

rustle *verb* **rustles, rustling, rustled**
To **rustle** means to make a gentle sound like the wind blowing through dry leaves.

Dictionary fun

Which words are compound words (can be split into smaller words)?

? ? ? ?

Ss

sack *noun* **sacks**
A **sack** is a large bag made of strong material.

sad *adjective*
Someone who is unhappy is **sad**.

saddle *noun* **saddles**
A **saddle** is a seat for the rider of a bicycle or a horse.

safari *noun* **safaris**
A **safari** is an expedition to look at or hunt wild animals such as lions.

safe *noun* **safes**
A **safe** is a strong box in which valuable things and money can be locked away.

safe *adjective*
Someone who is free from danger is **safe**.

sail *noun* **sails**
A **sail** is a large piece of material joined to the mast of a boat used to help the wind blow the boat along.

sail *verb* **sails, sailing, sailed**
To **sail** means to travel in a boat.

sailor *noun* **sailors**
A **sailor** is someone who works on a boat or ship.

salad *noun* **salads**
A **salad** is a mixture of raw or cold vegetables.

sale *noun* **sales**
1. A **sale** is the selling of something.
2. A **sale** is a time when things in a shop are sold at lower prices.

salt *noun* **salts**
Salt is a white grain used to flavour food.

same *adjective*
When two things are not different, they are the **same**.

sand *noun*
Sand is tiny grains of stone found in deserts or on the edge of the sea.

sandal *noun* **sandals**
A **sandal** is a kind of open shoe with straps.

sandwich *noun* **sandwiches**
A **sandwich** is two slices of bread and butter with another food between them.

sap *noun*
Sap is the liquid inside a plant.

satellite *noun* **satellites**
A **satellite** is something that moves in space around a planet.

sauce *noun* **sauces**
A **sauce** is a liquid added to or poured over food for flavouring.

saucer *noun* **saucers**
A **saucer** is a kind of small plate used to put a cup on.

sausage *noun* **sausages**
A **sausage** is a skin tube, usually filled with minced meat and other ingredients.

save *verb* **saves, saving, saved**
1. To **save** means to rescue someone or something from danger.
2. To **save** means to keep money or something else for use later.

saw *noun* **saws**
A **saw** is a tool with sharp teeth for cutting wood.

saw *verb*
This is the past tense of the verb 'to see' (see **see**).

say *verb* **says, saying, said**
To **say** means to speak.

scald *verb* **scalds, scalding, scalded**
To **scald** means to injure with hot liquid or steam.

scale *noun* **scales**
1. A **scale** is the set of marks used for measuring on instruments such as rulers or thermometers.
2. A **scale** is a set of musical notes going up or down one step at a time.

scales *noun* **scales**
1. **Scales** are an instrument for weighing things.
2. **Scales** are thin flakes covering fish and some other creatures.

Dictionary fun

Which word rhymes with **hail**?

? **?** ? ?

scar *noun* **scars**
A **scar** is the mark left on the skin after a cut has healed.

scare *verb* **scares, scaring, scared**
To **scare** means to frighten.

scarf *noun* **scarves**
A **scarf** is a strip of material worn round the neck or head.

scatter *verb* **scatters, scattering, scattered**
To **scatter** means to throw several things in different directions.

scene *noun* **scenes**
1. A **scene** is the place where something has happened.
2. A **scene** is part of a play.

scent *noun* **scents**
1. A **scent** is a smell.
2. **Scent** is a liquid with a very pleasant smell.

school *noun* **schools**
A **school** is a place where children go to learn.

science *noun* **sciences**
Science is knowledge about the way things in nature work.

scientist *noun* **scientists**
A **scientist** is someone who studies science.

scissors *noun* **scissors**
Scissors are a tool of two sharp blades  joined together and used for cutting things.

score *noun* **scores**
A **score** is the number of points gained by each side in a game.

score *verb* **scores, scoring, scored**
To **score** means to get a point or goal in a game.

scorpion *noun* **scorpions**
A **scorpion** is a kind of spider with a poisonous sting in its tail.

scramble *verb* **scrambles, scrambling, scrambled**
To **scramble** means to climb awkwardly using hands and feet.

scrap *noun* **scraps**
1. A **scrap** is a small piece of something.
2. **Scrap** is rubbish.

scrape *verb* **scrapes, scraping, scraped**
To **scrape** means to rub on something rough.

scratch *verb* **scratches, scratching, scratched**
1. To **scratch** means to rub something using nails or a sharp object.
2. To **scratch** means to rub or scrape the skin when it itches.

scream *verb* **screams, screaming, screamed**
To **scream** means to make a loud cry because of fear or pain.

screen *noun* **screens**
1. A **screen** is a smooth surface on which films, television programmes and the output from a computer are shown.
2. A **screen** is a covered framework used to hide things or protect people from draughts or heat.

screw *noun* **screws**
A **screw** is a kind of nail with grooves that is turned to fasten things together.

screw *verb* **screws, screwing, screwed**
To **screw** means to turn or twist something.

scribble *verb* **scribbles, scribbling, scribbled**
To **scribble** means to write or draw untidily.

scrub *verb* **scrubs, scrubbing, scrubbed**
To **scrub** means to rub something hard to clean it.

sea *noun* **seas**
A **sea** is a very large area of salt water.

seal *noun* **seals**
A **seal** is a furry mammal that lives in the sea and on land.

seal *verb* **seals, sealing, sealed**
To **seal** means to close something tightly.

search *verb* **searches, searching, searched**
To **search** means to look for something.

Dictionary fun

Which words (on this page) have a silent **c**?

?

season *noun* **seasons**
A **season** is one part of the year. Most parts of the world have four seasons: spring, summer, autumn and winter. Some parts have two, a wet and dry season.

seat *noun* **seats**
A **seat** is something to sit on.

seaweed *noun*
Seaweed is a plant that grows in the sea.

secret *noun* **secrets**
A **secret** is something that must not be said or shown to other people.

secretary *noun* **secretaries**
A **secretary** is someone who writes letters, answers the telephone, looks after papers and makes arrangements for other people.

see *verb* **sees, seeing, saw, seen**
To **see** means to use the eyes to look at things.

see-saw *noun* **see-saws**
A **see-saw** is a piece of playground equipment that is plank balanced in the middle, on which two people sit on the ends and make it go up and down.

seed *noun* **seeds**
A **seed** is a tiny part of a plant that can grow into a new plant when planted.

seem *verb* **seems, seeming, seemed**
To **seem** means to appear to be something.

selfish *adjective*
Someone who only thinks about himself or herself is **selfish**.

sell *verb* **sells, selling, sold**
To **sell** means to give something in exchange for money.

send *verb* **sends, sending, sent**
To **send** means to make someone or something go somewhere.

sense *noun* **senses**
1. A **sense** is the power to see, hear, smell, feel or taste.
2. A **sense** is a feeling about something.

sensible *adjective*
Someone who makes good decisions is **sensible**.

sentence *noun* **sentences**
A **sentence** is a group of words belonging together.

separate *adjective*
Things that are not joined together are **separate**.

series *noun* **series**
1. A **series** is a full set of something.
2. A **series** is a number of things that come one after another.

serious *adjective*
1. Something that is not funny is **serious**.
2. Someone who is thoughtful and careful is **serious**.
3. Something that is very bad is **serious**.

serve *verb* **serves, serving, served**
1. To **serve** means to sell things to people.
2. To **serve** means to work for someone or to give food to someone at a meal.

set *noun* **sets**
A **set** is a group of things or people that belong together.

set *verb* **sets, setting, set**
1. To **set** means to put or arrange things.
2. To **set** means to become hard or solid.

several *noun and adjective*
Several is more than two but not very many.

sew *verb* **sews, sewing, sewed, sewn**
To **sew** means to join pieces of material together using a needle and thread.

shade *noun* **shades**
1. **Shade** is a place with no direct sunlight.
2. A **shade** is the depth of a colour.

shade *verb* **shades, shading, shaded**
1. To **shade** means to keep strong sunlight away from something.
2. To **shade** means to darken parts of a picture.

Dictionary fun

What two other words sound like **sew**, but are spelled differently?

? ? ? ?

a b c d e f g h i j k l m n o p q r **s** t u v w x y z

shadow *noun* **shadows**
A **shadow** is the darkness that appears near something when the light is blocked.

shake *verb* **shakes, shaking, shook, shaken**
To **shake** means to move something up and down or from side to side quickly.

shallow *adjective*
Something that is not deep is **shallow**.

shame *noun*
Shame is a guilty feeling because of doing something wrong.

shampoo *noun* **shampoos**
A **shampoo** is a liquid soap for washing hair.

shape *noun* **shapes**
A **shape** is the outline of something.

share *verb* **shares, sharing, shared**
1. To **share** means to divide something into parts and give them to other people.
2. To **share** means to use something that someone else is also using.

shark *noun* **sharks**
A **shark** is a large sea fish with sharp teeth.

sharp *adjective*
1. Something that has a thin cutting edge or point is **sharp**.
2. Someone who is clever and quick to notice things is **sharp**.
3. Something that is sudden is **sharp**.

sharpen *verb* **sharpens, sharpening, sharpened**
To **sharpen** means to make something sharper.

shave *verb* **shaves, shaving, shaved**
To **shave** means to make the skin smooth by cutting off the hair using a blade.

she *pronoun*
She is the female person or animal being discussed.

shed *noun* **sheds**
A **shed** is a small hut.

shed *verb* **sheds, shedding, shed**
To **shed** means to let something fall off.

sheep *noun* **sheep**
A **sheep** is a farm animal kept for its wool and meat.

sheet *noun* **sheets**
1. A **sheet** is a piece of cloth put on a bed.
2. A **sheet** is a flat, thin piece of something, such as paper or glass.

shelf *noun* **shelves**
A **shelf** is a long piece of wood, glass or metal fixed to a wall for putting things on.

shell *noun* **shells**
A **shell** is the hard outer covering on an egg, nut and some animals.

shelter *noun* **shelters**
A **shelter** is a place which gives protection from the weather or from danger.

shield *noun* **shields**
A **shield** is a large piece of metal, leather or plastic held in front of the body to protect it.

shine *verb* **shines, shining, shone**
To **shine** means to give out light or to be bright.

ship *noun* **ships**
A **ship** is a large boat used to take people and things across the sea.

shirt *noun* **shirts**
A **shirt** is a piece of clothing worn on the top half of the body.

shiver *verb* **shivers, shivering, shivered**
To **shiver** means to shake with cold or fear.

shock *noun* **shocks**
A **shock** is an unexpected, unpleasant surprise.

shoe *noun* **shoes**
A **shoe** is a strong outer covering worn on the foot.

shoot *noun* **shoots**
A **shoot** is the new tip of a growing plant.

shoot *verb* **shoots, shooting, shot**
1. To **shoot** means to use a gun.
2. To **shoot** means to wound or kill someone by shooting.
3. To **shoot** means to move very quickly.

Dictionary fun

Which word rhymes with **pear**?

? ? ? ?

shop *noun* **shops**
A **shop** is a building where people can buy things.

shop *verb* **shops, shopping, shopped**
To **shop** means to buy things from shops.

shore *noun* **shores**
A **shore** is the land at the edge of the sea or a lake.

short *adjective*
1. Something that is not long is **short**.
2. Someone who is not tall is **short**.

shot *noun* **shots**
A **shot** is the firing of a gun.

should *verb*
Should means ought to.

shoulder *noun* **shoulders**
A **shoulder** is the part of the body between the arm and the neck.

shout *verb* **shouts, shouting, shouted**
To **shout** means to speak very loudly.

shovel *noun* **shovels**
A **shovel** is a tool for moving things, such as sand, soil or snow. It has a curved blade.

show *noun* **shows**
1. A **show** is an entertainment.
2. A **show** is a display or exhibition.

show *verb* **shows, showing, showed, shown**
1. To **show** means to let something be seen.
2. To **show** means to point out or make something clear to someone.

shower *noun* **showers**
1. A **shower** is a short fall of rain or snow.
2. A **shower** is something falling like rain, such as leaves.
3. A **shower** is a device that sprays water and is used to wash the body.

shut *verb* **shuts, shutting, shut**
To **shut** means to move a door, lid or cover so that an opening is blocked up.

shy *adjective*
Someone who does not like meeting others because of fear or fright is **shy**.

sick *adjective*
Someone who is ill is **sick**.

side *noun* **sides**
1. A **side** is a flat or fairly flat surface of something.
2. A **side** is an edge of something.
3. A **side** is an outer part of someone or something, between the front and the back.
4. A **side** is a group of people playing or fighting against another group.

sigh *verb* **sighs, sighing, sighed**
To **sigh** means to make a sound by breathing out heavily. Sometimes it is caused by sadness or relief.

sight *noun* **sights**
1. **Sight** is the ability to see.
2. A **sight** is something that can be seen.

sign *noun* **signs**
A **sign** is a mark, sound or action which means something special.

sign *verb* **signs, signing, signed**
1. To **sign** means to write your name.
2. To **sign** means to use movements of the hand to communicate.

silence *noun* **silences**
A **silence** is a time when there is no sound.

silent *adjective*
Someone or something that is making no sound is **silent**.

silly *adjective*
Someone who is foolish or thoughtless is **silly**.

silver *noun*
Silver is a valuable, white metal.

similar *adjective*
Something that is like another thing is **similar**.

simple *adjective*
1. Something that is easy or not complicated, is **simple**.
2. Something that is plain is **simple**.

Dictionary fun
Which word is the opposite of **different**?

? **?** **?** **?**

since *preposition*
The time after a certain point in time is **since** that point. *The weather has been warmer since April.*

since *conjunction*
Since means because. *The cricket match was cancelled since it rained all morning.*

sincerely *adverb*
When someone speaks honestly, he or she speaks **sincerely**.

sing *verb* **sings, singing, sang, sung**
To **sing** means to make a tune with the voice.

singer *noun* **singers**
A **singer** is someone who sings.

single *adjective*
1. When there is only one thing, there is a **single** thing.
2. Someone who is not married is **single**.

singular *adjective*
When there is one of something, it is **singular**.

sink *noun* **sinks**
A **sink** is a basin with taps where the washing-up is done.

sink *verb* **sinks, sinking, sank, sunk**
To **sink** means to go down or to go under water.

sip *verb* **sips, sipping, sipped**
To **sip** means to drink taking a tiny amount at a time.

siren *noun* **sirens**
A **siren** is a machine which makes a loud sound as a warning.

sister *noun* **sisters**
A **sister** is a girl or woman with the same parents as someone else.

sit *verb* **sits, sitting, sat**
To **sit** means to rest so that the bottom is supported.

size *noun* **sizes**
1. **Size** is how big something is.
2. A **size** is a particular measurement.

skate *noun* **skates**
A **skate** is a boot with a metal blade at the bottom, used to move on ice.

skate *verb* **skates, skating, skated**
To **skate** means to move smoothly on skates.

skateboard *noun* **skateboards**
A **skateboard** is a piece of wood or plastic on wheels used to stand on while moving.

skeleton *noun* **skeletons**
A **skeleton** is the framework of bones in the body.

ski *noun* **skis**
A **ski** is a long piece of metal and plastic strapped to the foot for sliding over snow.

skid *verb* **skids, skidding, skidded**
To **skid** means to slide accidentally.

skilful *adjective*
Someone who can do something well and carefully is **skilful**.

skill *noun* **skills**
A **skill** is the ability to do something well.

skin *noun* **skins**
Skin is the outer layer of the body of a person or animal, or of a fruit or vegetable.

skip *verb* **skips, skipping, skipped**
1. To **skip** means to move along hopping from one foot to the other.
2. To **skip** means to jump over a rope that is being turned round and round.
3. To **skip** means to leave something out.

skirt *noun* **skirts**
A **skirt** is a piece of woman's clothing that hangs from the waist.

skull *noun* **skulls**
A **skull** is the bony framework in the head.

sky *noun* **skies**
The **sky** is the space overhead when outside.

skyscraper *noun* **skyscrapers**
A **skyscraper** is a very tall building.

slam *verb* **slams, slamming, slammed**
To **slam** means to close something very noisily.

Dictionary fun

Which word contains another word that means not well?

?

85

a b c d e f g h i j k l m n o p q r s t u v w x y z

slate *noun* **slates**
A **slate** is one of the thin pieces of grey rock used to cover a roof.

sledge (sled) *noun*
sledges (sleds)
A **sledge** is a flat vehicle with runners instead of wheels used for travelling over snow.

sleep *verb* **sleeps, sleeping, slept**
To **sleep** means to rest completely with eyes closed, as people do each night.

sleet *noun*
Sleet is a mixture of rain and snow.

sleeve *noun* **sleeves**
A **sleeve** is the part of a piece of clothing that covers the arm.

slice *noun* **slices**
A **slice** is a thin piece cut off something.

slide *noun* **slides**
1. A **slide** is a smooth, slippery surface on which people can slip or move smoothly.
2. A **slide** is a small photograph that can be shown on a screen.

slide *verb* **slides, sliding, slid**
To **slide** means to move smoothly and quickly over something.

slight *adjective*
1. Something that is small or unimportant is **slight**.
2. Someone who is thin is **slight**.

slim *verb* **slims, slimming, slimmed**
To **slim** means to try to get thinner.

slim *adjective*
Someone who is thin is **slim**.

slip *noun* **slips**
A **slip** is a small mistake.

slip *verb* **slips, slipping, slipped**
1. To **slip** means to slide suddenly.
2. To **slip** means to move away quietly and quickly.

slipper *noun* **slippers**
Slippers are soft, comfortable shoes worn indoors.

slope *noun* **slopes**
A **slope** is ground that goes upwards or downwards gradually.

slope *verb* **slopes, sloping, sloped**
To **slope** means to slant or be on an angle.

slot *noun* **slots**
A **slot** is a narrow opening.

slow *adjective*
1. Something that takes a long time is **slow**.
2. A clock that is behind the correct time is **slow**.

smack *verb* **smacks, smacking, smacked**
To **smack** means to hit someone with the palm of the hand.

small *adjective*
Something that is little is **small**.

smash *verb* **smashes, smashing, smashed**
To **smash** means to break into tiny pieces noisily.

smell *noun* **smells**
A **smell** is anything that can be smelled.

smell *verb* **smells, smelling, smelled or smelt**
To **smell** means to use the nose to find out something.

smile *verb* **smiles, smiling, smiled**
To **smile** means to show by the face that someone is happy, amused or friendly.

smoke *noun*
Smoke is the white or grey gas that goes up from a fire.

smoke *verb* **smokes, smoking, smoked**
To **smoke** means to take in tobacco smoke through the mouth and breathe it out.

smooth *adjective*
Something that has no lumps or rough parts is **smooth**.

snack *noun* **snacks**
A **snack** is a small meal.

snail *noun* **snails**
A **snail** is a soft, small creature with a shell on its back.

Dictionary fun
With which word can you move the first letter to the end to make a word meaning many?

? ? ? ?

snake *noun* **snakes**
A **snake** is a thin, long reptile with no legs.

snap *verb* **snaps, snapping, snapped**
1. To **snap** means to break suddenly.
2. To **snap** means to take a sudden bite.

sneeze *verb* **sneezes, sneezing, sneezed**
To **sneeze** means to make a sudden noise as air rushes out of the nose and mouth.

sniff *verb* **sniffs, sniffing, sniffed**
To **sniff** means to take in air noisily through the nose.

snore *verb* **snores, snoring, snored**
To **snore** means to breathe very noisily while asleep.

snorkel *noun* **snorkels**
A **snorkel** is a tube that someone breathes through under water.

snow *noun*
Snow is small, white flakes of frozen water which fall from clouds in very cold weather.

snowman *noun* **snowmen**
A **snowman** is a model of a person made out of snow.

soak *verb* **soaks, soaking, soaked**
To **soak** means to make something very wet.

soap *noun* **soaps**
Soap is something used with water for washing.

sock *noun* **socks**
A **sock** is a soft covering for the foot.

sofa *noun* **sofas**
A **sofa** is a comfortable seat with a back for more than one person.

soft *adjective*
1. Something that is not hard or firm is **soft**.
2. A sound that is not at all loud is **soft**.

soil *noun*
Soil is the top layer of the earth in which plants grow.

soldier *noun* **soldiers**
A **soldier** is a person in the army.

sole *noun* **soles**
1. A **sole** is the bottom part of a foot or shoe.
2. A **sole** is a flat sea fish.

solid *adjective*
1. Something that is not hollow is **solid**.
2. Something that is hard and firm is **solid**.

some *adjective*
1. When there is a little or a few of something, there is **some** of it.
2. When one of an unknown thing did something, **some** thing did it.

song *noun* **songs**
A **song** is music with words that are sung.

soon *adverb*
Something that will be done in a short time from now will be done **soon**.

soot *noun*
Soot is a black powder left by smoke.

sore *adjective*
A part of the body that is painful is **sore**.

sorry *adjective*
Someone who feels sad because of something wrong he or she did, or that has happened to another person, is **sorry**.

sound *noun* **sounds**
A **sound** is something that can be heard.

soup *noun* **soups**
Soup is a hot, liquid food usually made from meat or vegetables.

sour *adjective*
1. A taste that is bitter is **sour**.
2. Food that is not fresh, such as milk, is **sour**.

south *noun*
South is the direction opposite north.

souvenir *noun* **souvenirs**
A **souvenir** is something that reminds you of a place, person or event.

sow *verb* **sows, sowing, sowed, sown**
To **sow** means to plant seeds in the ground.

Dictionary fun
Which word rhymes with **poke**?

? **?** ? ?

space *noun* **spaces**
1. A **space** is the distance between things.
2. A **space** is an empty gap.
3. **Space** is all the area in which the planets and stars move.

spaceship *noun* **spaceships**
A **spaceship** is a vehicle that travels into space.

spade *noun* **spades**
1. A **spade** is a tool with a long handle used for digging.
2. A **spade** is a black shape on playing-cards.

spaghetti *noun*
Spaghetti is a long, thin form of pasta.

spark *noun* **sparks**
A **spark** is a small, bright flash.

sparkle *verb* **sparkles, sparkling, sparkled**
To **sparkle** means to shine with a lot of tiny sparks.

speak *verb* **speaks, speaking, spoke, spoken**
To **speak** means to use the voice to make words.

spear *noun* **spears**
A **spear** is a sharp, metal point on the end of a long pole, used as a weapon.

special *adjective*
1. Something that is unusual and different from others is **special**.
2. Something that is for a particular event or person is **special**.

speck *noun* **specks**
A **speck** is a tiny spot or piece of something.

speech *noun* **speeches**
1. **Speech** is the ability to speak.
2. A **speech** is a talk given to a group of people.

speed *noun* **speeds**
Speed is how quickly something moves.

spell *noun* **spells**
A **spell** is magic words said to make something happen in fairy tales.

spell *verb* **spells, spelling, spelled or spelt**
To **spell** means to put the letters of a word in the correct order.

spend *verb* **spends, spending, spent**
To **spend** means to pay out money for something.

sphere *noun* **spheres**
A **sphere** is a round shape like a ball.

spice *noun* **spices**
A **spice** is a substance from a plant used to flavour food.

spider *noun* **spiders**
A **spider** is a small creature with eight legs that spins webs.

spike *noun* **spikes**
A **spike** is a sharp, metal point.

spin *verb* **spins, spinning, spun**
1. To **spin** means to turn round quickly.
2. To **spin** means to twist wool or cotton into a thread.

spine *noun* **spines**
1. A **spine** is the long series of bones down the centre of the back.
2. A **spine** is a thorn or prickle.

splash *noun* **splashes**
A **splash** is liquid flying about because something has been dropped into it.

splash *verb* **splashes, splashing, splashed**
To **splash** means to make liquid fly about in drops.

splendid *adjective*
Something that looks very good or is excellent is **splendid**.

split *verb* **splits, splitting, split**
To **split** means to break something into pieces.

spoil *verb* **spoils, spoiling, spoilt**
1. To **spoil** means to make something less good or useful than it was before.
2. To **spoil** means to be too kind to a person so that he or she thinks that everything that is wanted can be had.

spoke *noun* **spokes**
A **spoke** is one of the wires or rods that joins the centre of a wheel to the rim.

Dictionary fun

Which word describes the gaps between these words?

? **?** ? ?

spoke *verb*
This is the past tense of the verb 'to speak' (see **speak**).

sponge *noun* **sponges**
1. A **sponge** is a light kind of cake.
2. A **sponge** is something light and soft with small holes in it. It is used for cleaning.

spoon *noun* **spoons**
A **spoon** is a small bowl on the end of a handle used for eating food.

sport *noun* **sports**
A **sport** is a game or amusement usually done outside, such as football or running.

spot *noun* **spots**
1. A **spot** is a small, round mark.
2. A **spot** is a place.
3. A **spot** is a small, raised, coloured mark on the skin.

spot *verb* **spots, spotting, spotted**
To **spot** means to notice something.

spout *noun* **spouts**
A **spout** is a pipe attached to a container used for pouring liquid out of it.

spray *verb* **sprays, spraying, sprayed**
To **spray** means to scatter tiny drops of liquid over something.

spread *verb* **spreads, spreading, spread**
To **spread** means to lay or stretch something out to its full size.

spring *noun* **springs**
1. A **spring** is a place where water flows out of the ground.
2. A **spring** is a piece of metal wound in rings so that it can stretch and then return to its normal shape.

spring *verb* **springs, springing, sprang, sprung**
To **spring** means to jump up suddenly.

sprint *verb* **sprints, sprinting, sprinted**
To **sprint** means to run very quickly over a small distance.

spy *noun* **spies**
A **spy** is a person who tries to find out secret information.

spy *verb* **spies, spying, spied**
To **spy** means to see something secret.

squash *noun*
Squash is an indoor game played with rackets and a small, rubber ball.

squash *verb* **squashes, squashing, squashed**
To **squash** means to crush something.

squeeze *verb* **squeezes, squeezing, squeezed**
To **squeeze** means to crush or press something hard.

squirrel *noun* **squirrels**
A **squirrel** is a small animal with a long, bushy tail that lives in trees.

stable *noun* **stables**
A **stable** is a building in which horses or cattle are kept and fed.

stack *noun* **stacks**
A **stack** is a pile or heap.

stage *noun* **stages**
1. A **stage** is a raised floor in a hall or theatre.
2. A **stage** is a point reached when someone is doing something.

stagecoach *noun* **stagecoaches**
A **stagecoach** is a horse-drawn coach which was used to carry people and things along a known route.

stain *noun* **stains**
A **stain** is an unwanted, dirty mark on something.

stairs *noun*
Stairs are a set of steps going from one floor to another in a building.

stale *adjective*
Something that is not fresh is **stale**.

stalk *noun* **stalks**
A **stalk** is a thin stem of a flower or plant.

Dictionary fun

Which word describes tennis, golf and swimming?

?

89

stamp *noun* **stamps**

A **stamp** is a small piece of coloured paper that is stuck on a letter or parcel before sending it, to show that payment is made.

stamp *verb* **stamps, stamping, stamped**

To **stamp** means to bang the foot heavily down on the ground.

stand *noun* **stands**

A **stand** is a support to rest things on or in.

stand *verb* **stands, standing, stood**

To **stand** means to be upright on the feet without moving.

star *noun* **stars**

1. A **star** is a tiny, bright light seen in the sky at night.
2. A **star** is a famous performer.

stare *verb* **stares, staring, stared**

To **stare** means to look at someone or something continuously.

starfish *noun*
starfishes or **starfish**

A **starfish** is a sea creature with a body shaped like a five-pointed star.

start *verb* **starts, starting, started**

1. To **start** means to begin something.
2. To **start** means to make something happen.

startle *verb* **startles, startling, startled**

To **startle** means to frighten someone by doing something unexpected.

starve *verb* **starves, starving, starved**

To **starve** means to become ill or die because of lack of food.

station *noun* **stations**

1. A **station** is a place with buildings where trains or buses stop.
2. A **station** is a building for police officers and firefighters.

statue *noun* **statues**

A **statue** is a model of a person made out of stone or metal.

stay *verb* **stays, staying, stayed**

1. To **stay** means to remain in the same place.
2. To **stay** means to live somewhere while visiting a place.

steady *adjective*

Something that is not shaking is **steady**.

steak *noun* **steaks**

A **steak** is a thick slice of meat or fish.

steal *verb* **steals, stealing, stole, stolen**

To **steal** means to take something that belongs to somebody else and keep it.

steam *noun*

Steam is the vapour that comes from boiling water.

steel *noun*

Steel is a strong metal made from iron.

steep *adjective*

Something that slopes sharply is **steep**.

steer *verb* **steers, steering, steered**

To **steer** means to control the direction in which something moves.

stem *noun* **stems**

1. A **stem** is the main part of a plant growing up from the ground.
2. A **stem** is the thin part of a plant that joins a leaf, flower or fruit to the rest of the plant.

step *noun* **steps**

1. A **step** is the movement made by one foot when walking.
2. A **step** is a flat place to put a foot when walking from one level to another.

stick *noun* **sticks**

A **stick** is a long, thin piece of wood.

stick *verb* **sticks, sticking, stuck**

1. To **stick** means to push a sharp point into something.
2. To **stick** means to fix something.

stiff *adjective*

Something that does not bend easily is **stiff**.

still *adjective*

Something that is not moving is **still**.

still *adverb*

When something is the same as it was, it is **still** like that.

Dictionary fun

Which word spelled backwards describes animals that are kept by people?

? **?** ? ?

sting *noun* **stings**
A **sting** or **stinger** is part of animal or plant that contains poison and hurts when touched.

sting *verb* **stings, stinging, stung**
To **sting** means to hurt someone with a sting.

stir *verb* **stirs, stirring, stirred**
1. To **stir** means to move a liquid or soft mixture round and round.
2. To **stir** means to move slightly.

stitch *noun* **stitches**
1. A **stitch** is a loop of thread made when sewing or knitting.
2. A **stitch** is a sharp pain in the side that sometimes happens when running.

stomach *noun* **stomachs**
A **stomach** is the part of the body where food goes when it has been swallowed.

stone *noun* **stones**
1. **Stone** is rock.
2. A **stone** is a piece of rock.
3. A **stone** is the large, hard seed in the middle of some fruits.

stool *noun* **stools**
A **stool** is a seat with no back.

stop *verb* **stops, stopping, stopped**
1. To **stop** means to end or come to rest.
3. To **stop** means to stay somewhere for a while.

store *noun* **stores**
A **store** is a large shop.

store *verb* **stores, storing, stored**
To **store** means to keep things in a safe place until they are needed.

storm *noun* **storms**
A **storm** is a time of very strong winds and heavy rain or snow.

story *noun* **stories**
A **story** is a collection of words which describe real or imaginary happenings.

stove *noun* **stoves**
A **stove** is an appliance used for heating or cooking.

straight *adjective*
Something that does not bend is **straight**.

strange *adjective*
Something that is unusual or not known before is **strange**.

stranger *noun* **strangers**
1. A **stranger** is someone who is not known to you.
2. A **stranger** is someone who is in a place he or she does not know.

straw *noun* **straws**
1. **Straw** is dry stalks of grains or grasses.
2. A **straw** is a thin tube for drinking through.

strawberry *noun* **strawberries**
A **strawberry** is a small, sweet fruit.

stream *noun* **streams**
A **stream** is a small river.

street *noun* **streets**
A **street** is a road in a town with buildings along it.

strength *noun* **strengths**
Strength tells how strong someone or something is.

stretch *verb* **stretches, stretching, stretched**
To **stretch** means to pull something so that it is longer or wider.

stride *verb* **strides, striding, strode**
To **stride** means to walk with long steps.

strike *verb* **strikes, striking, struck**
1. To **strike** means to hit something.
2. To **strike** means to stop work as a protest.

string *noun*
String is very thin rope or cord.

stripe *noun* **stripes**
A **stripe** is a long, narrow band of colour.

stroke *noun* **strokes**
A **stroke** is a hitting movement.

stroke *verb* **strokes, stroking, stroked**
To **stroke** means to move the hand gently along something.

Dictionary fun

Which word can mean the same as **odd**?

???

strong *adjective*
1. Someone or something that has a lot of power or is **strong** or is not easily broken.
2. Something that has a lot of flavour or taste is **strong**.

student *noun* **students**
A **student** is a person who is studying.

study *noun* **studies**
A **study** is a room where someone studies.

study *verb* **studies, studying, studied**
1. To **study** means to spend time learning about something.
2. To **study** means to look at something very carefully.

stumble *verb* **stumbles, stumbling, stumbled**
To **stumble** means to trip or almost fall over something.

stupid *adjective*
Someone or something that is very silly or does something foolish is **stupid**.

subject *noun* **subjects**
A **subject** is a person, thing or idea being talked, written or learnt about.

submarine *noun* **submarines**
A **submarine** is a type of ship that can travel under water.

subtract *verb* **subtracts, subtracting, subtracted**
To **subtract** means to take one number away from another.

succeed *verb* **succeeds, succeeding, succeeded**
To **succeed** means to do what you tried.

success *noun* **successes**
A **success** is something you suceed at doing.

such *adjective*
1. Things that are of a certain kind are **such** things.
2. An experience that was so great was **such** an experience.

suck *verb* **sucks, sucking, sucked**
1. To **suck** means to draw in liquid or air.
2. To **suck** means to keep something moving around in the mouth without biting it.

sudden *adjective*
Something that happens quickly and unexpectedly is **sudden**.

suddenly *adverb*
When something happens quickly and unexpectedly, it happens **suddenly**.

sugar *noun*
Sugar is a sweet-tasting food used to sweeten other foods.

suggest *verb* **suggests, suggesting, suggested**
To **suggest** means to give someone an idea.

suit *noun* **suits**
A **suit** is a jacket and a pair of trousers or a skirt, made out of the same material.

suit *verb* **suits, suiting, suited**
1. To **suit** means to be convenient for someone.
2. To **suit** means to look right on someone.

suitable *adjective*
Something that is what is wanted is **suitable**.

sum *noun* **sums**
1. A **sum** is the total when numbers are added together.
2. A **sum** is an amount of money.

Sun *noun*
The **Sun** is the star that gives the Earth heat and light.

sunny *adjective*
When the sun shines, it is **sunny**.

supermarket *noun* **supermarkets**
A **supermarket** is a large food store where people serve themselves and pay as they leave.

supper *noun* **suppers**
A **supper** is an evening meal or snack.

Dictionary fun
Which word could be white or brown?

? ? ? ?

support *verb* **supports, supporting, supported**
1. To **support** means to hold something up so that it does not fall over.
2. To **support** means to give help to someone.

sure *adjective*
Someone who is certain is **sure**.

surf *noun*
Surf is large, white waves breaking on the shore.

surface *noun* **surfaces**
1. A **surface** is the outside of something.
2. A **surface** is a flat area on the top or outside of something.

surprise *noun* **surprises**
1. A **surprise** is something that was not expected.
2. **Surprise** is the feeling when something unexpected happens.

surrender *verb* **surrenders, surrendering, surrendered**
To **surrender** means to stop fighting and give in to the enemy.

swallow *verb* **swallows, swallowing, swallowed**
To **swallow** means to make something go down your throat.

swamp *noun* **swamps**
A **swamp** is an area of very wet ground.

swarm *noun* **swarms**
A **swarm** is a large group of insects.

sweat *verb* **sweats, sweating, sweated**
To **sweat** means to give off liquid through the skin when hot or ill.

sweater *noun* **sweaters**
A **sweater** is a knitted piece of clothing worn on the upper part of the body.

sweep *verb* **sweeps, sweeping, swept**
To **sweep** means to clean using a brush or broom.

sweet *noun* **sweets**
A **sweet** is a small piece of food made with sugar or chocolate.

sweet *adjective*
1. Something that tastes of sugar is **sweet**.
2. Something that is very pleasant or attractive is **sweet**.

swell *verb* **swells, swelling, swelled, swollen**
To **swell** means to get bigger.

swerve *verb* **swerves, swerving, swerved**
To **swerve** means to change direction suddenly to avoid something while moving.

swift *adjective*
Someone or something that is quick is **swift**.

swim *verb* **swims, swimming, swam, swum**
1. To **swim** means to move the body through water.
2. To **swim** means to cross something by swimming.

swimmer *noun* **swimmers**
A **swimmer** is someone who is swimming.

swing *noun* **swings**
A **swing** is a seat hung from a bar or the branch of a tree for someone to swing on.

swing *verb* **swings, swinging, swung**
To **swing** means to move freely backwards and forwards or from side to side.

switch *noun* **switches**
A **switch** is a device for turning electricity on and off.

switch *verb* **switches, switching, switched**
To **switch** means to change suddenly from one thing to another.

sword *noun* **swords**
A **sword** is a weapon with a sharp blade.

symbol *noun* **symbols**
A **symbol** is a sign used to represent something.

synagogue *noun* **synagogues**
A **synagogue** is a building where Jewish people worship.

syrup *noun*
Syrup is very sweet, thick liquid.

Dictionary fun
Which word (on this page) has a silent **w**?

? **?** ? ?

Tt

table *noun* **tables**
1. A **table** is a piece of furniture with a flat top and legs.
2. A **table** is a list of information arranged in order.

tablespoon *noun* **tablespoons**
A **tablespoon** is a large spoon used to serve food.

tadpole *noun* **tadpoles**
A **tadpole** is a small creature that lives in the water and grows into a frog or toad.

tail *noun* **tails**
A **tail** is the part at the end of something, especially at the end of an animal's back.

tailor *noun* **tailors**
A **tailor** is a person whose job is to make clothes.

take *verb* **takes, taking, took, taken**
1. To **take** means to get hold of something.
2. To **take** means to carry something away.

talk *verb* **talks, talking, talked**
To **talk** means to speak to someone.

tall *adjective*
Someone or something that has a height higher than average is **tall**.

tambourine *noun* **tambourines**
A **tambourine** is a round, musical instrument that is shaken or hit with the fingers.

tame *adjective*
Something that is not wild or dangerous is **tame**.

tank *noun* **tanks**
1. A **tank** is a container for holding liquid.
2. A **tank** is a large, heavy, fighting vehicle.

tanker *noun* **tankers**
1. A **tanker** is a large vehicle for carrying liquid.
2. A **tanker** is a large ship for carrying oil.

tap *noun* **taps**
1. A **tap** is a device for controlling the flow of liquid or gas.
2. A **tap** is a gentle hit.

tap *verb* **taps, tapping, tapped**
To **tap** means to make quick, gentle hits.

tape *noun* **tapes**
1. A **tape** is a narrow strip of cloth, paper or plastic.
2. A **tape** is a narrow, plastic strip used to make sound or video recordings.

tar *noun*
Tar is a thick, black, sticky liquid used to make roads.

target *noun* **targets**
A **target** is something to be aimed at.

taste *noun* **tastes**
A **taste** is the flavour of something.

taste *verb* **tastes, tasting, tasted**
To **taste** means to put something in the mouth to see what its flavour is like.

taught *verb*
This is the past tense of the verb 'to teach' (see **teach**).

taxi *noun* **taxis**
A **taxi** is a vehicle for which someone pays the driver to be taken somewhere.

tea *noun* **teas**
1. **Tea** is a hot drink made from pouring boiling water on dried leaves.
2. **Tea** is a meal eaten in the afternoon.

teach *verb* **teaches, teaching, taught**
To **teach** means to help someone to understand or do something.

teacher *noun* **teachers**
A **teacher** is a person whose job is to teach.

Dictionary fun

Which words are compound words (can be split into smaller words)?

?

team *noun* **teams**
A **team** is a group of people who work together or play a game together on the same side.

teapot *noun* **teapots**
A **teapot** is a container with a spout and a lid used for making tea.

tear *noun* **tears**
A **tear** is a drop of liquid that comes out of the eye.

tear *verb* **tears, tearing, tore, torn**
To **tear** means to damage something by pulling it apart.

tease *verb* **teases, teasing, teased**
To **tease** means to annoy someone in a joking way.

teaspoon *noun* **teaspoons**
A **teaspoon** is a small spoon used for stirring tea.

teddy bear *noun* **teddy bears**
A **teddy bear** is a soft, furry, toy bear.

teenager *noun* **teenagers**
A **teenager** is someone whose age is between 13 and 19 years.

telephone *noun* **telephones**
A **telephone** is an instrument that allows sound to travel great distances so that one person can speak to another person a long way away.

telephone *verb* **telephones, telephoning, telephoned**
To **telephone** means to speak to someone through a telephone.

telescope *noun* **telescopes**
A **telescope** is an instrument with lenses in it which allows someone to see things that are far away.

television *noun* **televisions**
A **television** is a machine which picks up electronic signals sent through the air and changes them into pictures and sound.

tell *verb* **tells, telling, told**
To **tell** means to speak in order to pass on information.

temper *noun* **tempers**
A **temper** is a mood.

temperature *noun* **temperatures**
A **temperature** is a measurement of how hot or cold something is.

temple *noun* **temples**
A **temple** is a building where people worship.

tender *adjective*
1. Something that is delicate is **tender**.
2. Something that is soft or easily chewed is **tender**.
3. Someone who is loving is **tender**.

tennis *noun*
Tennis is a game where a ball is hit over a net.

tense *adjective*
1. Someone who is nervous and strained is **tense**.
2. Something that has been tightly stretched is **tense**.

tent *noun* **tents**
A **tent** is a shelter made out of canvas or nylon and used for camping.

term *noun* **terms**
A **term** is a period of time, such as when a school, college or university is open.

terrible *adjective*
Something that is very bad is **terrible**.

terrify *verb* **terrifies, terrifying, terrified**
To **terrify** means to frighten someone very badly.

Dictionary fun

What two letters are a shortened version of television?

? **?** ? ?

terror *noun* **terrors**
Terror is great fear.

test *noun* **tests**
A **test** is a set of questions to find out what someone knows or can do.

test *verb* **tests, testing, tested**
To **test** means to try something out.

than *conjunction*
Than is a word used when comparing two things. *Jack is taller than Jill.*

thank *verb* **thanks, thanking, thanked**
To **thank** means to say that you are grateful to someone.

theatre *noun* **theatres**
A **theatre** is a place where people can watch plays or movies.

their *pronoun*
Their means belonging to them.

these *pronoun*
The things near here are **these** things.

they *pronoun*
They are the people or things being talked about.

thick *adjective*
Something that is not thin but measures a lot from one side to the other is **thick**.

thief *noun* **thieves**
A **thief** is someone who steals something.

thimble *noun* **thimbles**
A **thimble** is a cover for the end of the finger worn to protect it when sewing.

thin *adjective*
Someone or something that is not thick or fat is **thin**.

thing *noun* **things**
A **thing** is anything that can be seen or touched.

think *verb* **thinks, thinking, thought**
To **think** is to use the mind to form an idea.

third *noun* **thirds**
A **third** is one of three equal parts into which something can be divided.

third *adjective*
Something coming after the second is **third**.

thirsty *adjective*
Someone who wants a drink is **thirsty**.

thistle *noun* **thistles**
A **thistle** is a wild plant with prickly leaves.

thorn *noun* **thorns**
A **thorn** is a sharp spike that grows on the stem of some plants.

those *pronoun*
The things there are **those** things.

though *conjunction*
Though means but, or in spite of the fact that. *The sky became very black though it did not rain.*

thought *noun* **thoughts**
A **thought** is an idea.

thought *verb*
This is the past tense of the verb 'to think' (see **think**).

thousand *noun* **thousands**
A **thousand** is the number 1000.

thread *noun* **threads**
A **thread** is a long, thin piece of cotton, wool or nylon used for sewing or weaving.

thread *verb* **threads, threading, threaded**
To **thread** means to put a piece of thread through the eye of a needle.

threw *verb*
This is the past tense of the verb 'to throw' (see **throw**).

throat *noun* **throats**
The **throat** is the front of the neck and the tube inside it, down which food and air pass.

through *preposition*
Someone or something that goes from one side or end to the other goes **through** it. *The baby slept all through the night.*

Dictionary fun

Which word describes the number of years in a millennium?

? **?** ? ?

throw *verb* **throws, throwing, threw, thrown**
To **throw** means to use the arm to make something move through the air.

thrush noun **thrushes**
A **thrush** is a bird with a speckled breast.

thumb *noun* **thumbs**
A **thumb** is the short, thick finger that grows from the side of the hand.

thunder *noun*
Thunder is the loud, crashing sound heard after lightning in a storm.

tick *noun* **ticks**
A **tick** is a mark often made when something is correct.

tick *verb* **ticks, ticking, ticked**
To **tick** means to make the sound of a clock.

ticket *noun* **tickets**
A **ticket** is a small piece of paper or card bought to allow someone to travel on a public vehicle or get into some places.

tickle *verb* **tickles, tickling, tickled**
To **tickle** means to touch the skin very lightly so that the person laughs.

tide *noun* **tides**
A **tide** is the slow movement of the sea up and down the shore.

tidy *adjective*
Things that are neatly arranged are **tidy**.

tie *noun* **ties**
A **tie** is a strip of material worn under the collar of a shirt and tied in a knot at the neck.

tie *verb* **ties, tying, tied**
To **tie** means to fasten with a knot.

tiger *noun* **tigers**
A **tiger** is a big, wild animal of the cat family that has yellow or orange fur with black stripes.

tight *adjective*
Something that fits or is fastened very closely is **tight**.

till *noun* **tills**
A **till** is a drawer for money in a shop.

till *preposition* and *conjunction*
Till means until. *She waited till it was warmer before going swimming.*

timber *noun*
Timber is wood that is ready to be used to make things.

time *noun* **times**
1. **Time** is the passing of seconds, minutes, days or years.
2. **Time** is a certain moment in time.
3. A **time** is the speed and rhythm of a piece of music.

timetable *noun* **timetables**
A **timetable** is a table showing when things will happen, such as when public vehicles will arrive and leave.

timid *adjective*
Someone who is not brave is **timid**.

tin *noun* **tins**
1. **Tin** is a soft, grey metal.
2. A **tin** is a metal container.

tinkle *verb* **tinkles, tinkling, tinkled**
To **tinkle** means to make soft, ringing sounds.

tinsel *noun*
Tinsel is shiny, silver ribbon used for decoration, especially at Christmas.

tiny *adjective*
Something that is very small is **tiny**.

tip *noun* **tips**
1. A **tip** is the very end of something.
2. A **tip** is a small present of money given to someone for doing something.

tip *verb* **tips, tipping, tipped**
To **tip** means to overturn something.

Dictionary fun

Which word could be found out by the use of a clock, watch or the sun?

? ? ? ?

tiptoe *verb* **tiptoes, tiptoeing, tiptoed**
To **tiptoe** means to walk on the toes silently.

tired *adjective*
Someone who feels the need to rest or is bored is **tired**.

tissue *noun* **tissues**
A **tissue** is a piece of soft, thin paper.

title *noun* **titles**
1. A **title** is the name of a book, play, film, picture or piece of music.
2. A **title** is a word that is put in front of a person's name, such as Mrs. or Dr.

to *preposition*
To means in the direction of. *She ran to the gate.*

toad *noun* **toads**
A **toad** is a creature like a large frog that has bumpy, dry skin.

toadstool *noun* **toadstools**
A **toadstool** is a kind of fungus like a mushroom. They are usually poisonous.

toast *noun*
Toast is bread that is heated so that it is crisp and brown.

today *noun*
Today is the day now.

toddler *noun* **toddlers**
A **toddler** is a young child who is learning to walk.

toe *noun* **toes**
A **toe** is one of the five parts at the end of the foot.

toffee *noun* **toffees**
A **toffee** is a small sweet made from butter and sugar.

together *adverb*
When someone is with someone else, they are **together**.

toilet *noun* **toilets**
A **toilet** is where people get rid of waste from their bodies.

told *verb*
This is the past tense of the verb 'to tell' (see **tell**).

tomato *noun* **tomatoes**
A **tomato** is a soft, juicy, round, red fruit.

tomorrow *noun*
Tomorrow is the day after today.

tongue *noun* **tongues**
A **tongue** is the long, soft part inside the mouth which moves when speaking or eating.

tonight *noun*
Tonight is this night.

tonne *noun* **tonnes**
A **tonne** is a unit of weight equal to 1000 kilograms.

too *adverb*
1. **Too** means also.
2. When there is more than is needed, there is **too** much.

took *verb*
This is the past tense of the verb 'to take' (see **take**).

tool *noun* **tools**
A **tool** is an instrument used to do a job.

tooth *noun* **teeth**
A **tooth** is one of the hard, white parts of the mouth used for biting.

toothache *noun*
Toothache is a pain in the tooth.

toothbrush *noun* **toothbrushes**
A **toothbrush** is a small brush with a long handle used for cleaning teeth.

toothpaste *noun*
Toothpaste is a paste put on a toothbrush to clean teeth.

Dictionary fun

Which other words sound the same as **too** but have different meanings and spellings?

? **?** **?** **?**

top *noun* **tops**
1. The **top** is the highest part of something.
2. A **top** is a toy that spins around very quickly.

tore *verb*
This is the past tense of the verb 'to tear' (see **tear**).

toss *verb* **tosses, tossing, tossed**
To **toss** means to throw.

total *noun* **totals**
A **total** is the amount when everything has been added up.

touch *verb* **touches, touching, touched**
1. To **touch** means to be in contact with something.
2. To **touch** means to affect someone's feelings. *Simon was touched by the boy's sad story.*

tough *adjective*
1. Something that is strong is **tough**.
2. Something that is hard to cut or chew is **tough**.

tourist *noun* **tourists**
A **tourist** is someone who is travelling on holiday.

tow *verb* **tows, towing, towed**
To **tow** means to pull something along.

towards *preposition*
Towards means in the direction of something. *She moved towards the fire because she was cold.*

towel *noun* **towels**
A **towel** is a piece of cloth for drying things.

tower *noun* **towers**
A **tower** is a tall, narrow building or part of a building.

town *noun* **towns**
A **town** is a place with houses, shops, schools and offices.

toy *noun* **toys**
A **toy** is something to play with.

track *noun* **tracks**
1. A **track** is a kind of path.
2. A **track** is a set of railway lines.
3. A **track** is a mark or footprint left by someone or something.

track *verb* **tracks, tracking, tracked**
To **track** means to follow the marks left by someone or something.

tractor *noun* **tractors**
A **tractor** is a vehicle used on farms.

trade *noun* **trades**
Trade is the buying and selling of goods.

traffic *noun*
Traffic is vehicles travelling on the road.

trail *noun* **trails**
A **trail** is a track.

trail *verb* **trails, trailing, trailed**
To **trail** means to drag along behind.

train *noun* **trains**
A **train** is a group of railway cars pulled by an engine along a railway track.

train *verb* **trains, training, trained**
1. To **train** means to teach a person or animal to do something.
2. To **train** means to practise doing something.

trampoline *noun* **trampolines**
A **trampoline** is a large piece of canvas attached to a frame on which people bounce up and down.

translate *verb* **translates, translating, translated**
To **translate** means to give the meaning of something written or spoken in another language.

Dictionary fun

What letter does the **gh** in tough sound like?

? **?** ? ?

transparent *adjective*
Something that is clear enough to see through is **transparent**.

trap *noun* **traps**
A **trap** is something made for catching animals.

trap *verb* **traps, trapping, trapped**
To **trap** means to catch something in a trap or by a clever trick.

trapdoor *noun* **trapdoors**
A **trapdoor** is a small door in a floor or ceiling.

trapeze *noun*
A **trapeze** is a bar hanging from two ropes for acrobats to swing on.

travel *verb* **travels, travelling, travelled**
To **travel** means to move from one place to another.

traveller *noun* **travellers**
A **traveller** is someone who travels around.

tray *noun* **trays**
A **tray** is a flat surface with a raised edge used for carrying things such as cups and saucers.

treasure *noun* **treasures**
Treasure is a collection of valuable objects, such as gold, jewels or money.

tree *noun* **trees**
A **tree** is a tall plant with a trunk and branches.

tremble *verb* **trembles, trembling, trembled**
To **tremble** means to shake because of cold or fright.

triangle *noun* **triangles**
A **triangle** is a shape with three straight sides.

trick *noun* **tricks**
A **trick** is a clever way that a person or animal has learned to do something.

trick *verb* **tricks, tricking, tricked**
To **trick** means to make someone believe something that is not true or did not happen.

tricycle *noun* **tricycles**
A **tricycle** is a vehicle with three wheels and pedals, often ridden by young children.

trigger *noun* **triggers**
A **trigger** is the part of a gun someone pulls to fire it.

trip *noun* **trips**
A **trip** is a journey or outing.

trip *verb* **trips, tripping, tripped**
To **trip** means to stumble or fall over something.

trouble *noun* **troubles**
A **trouble** is a difficulty or worry.

trouble *verb* **troubles, troubling, troubled**
1. To **trouble** means to worry someone.
2. To **trouble** someone means to cause them to do extra work.

trousers *noun* **trousers**
Trousers are a piece of clothing with two legs worn on the lower part of the body.

truck *noun* **trucks**
A **truck** is a large vehicle for carrying things.

true *adjective*
Something that is correct or real is **true**.

trumpet *noun* **trumpets**
A **trumpet** is a brass musical instrument.

trunk *noun* **trunks**
1. A **trunk** is the thick stem of a tree.
2. A **trunk** is a very large case.
3. A **trunk** is an elephant's long nose.

trust *verb* **trusts, trusting, trusted**
To **trust** means to believe that someone will be honest and not let you down.

truth *noun* **truths**
A **truth** is something that is true.

Dictionary fun

Which words start with **tri**, which stands for three?

a b c d e f g h i j k l m n o p q r s t u v w x y z

try *verb* **tries, trying, tried**
1. To **try** means to make an effort to do something.
2. To **try** means to test something to see how it works.

tube *noun* **tubes**
1. A **tube** is a hollow length of some material like a pipe.
2. A **tube** is a long, narrow container.

tug *noun* **tugs**
A **tug** is a boat for pulling ships.

tug *verb* **tugs, tugging, tugged**
To **tug** means to pull hard.

tulip *noun* **tulips**
A **tulip** is a spring flower that grows from a bulb.

tumble *verb* **tumbles, tumbling, tumbled**
To **tumble** means to fall.

tuna *noun* **tuna**
A **tuna** is a large fish that lives in the sea.

tunnel *noun* **tunnels**
A **tunnel** is a passage made through a hill or under a road or river.

turban *noun* **turbans**
A **turban** is a covering for the head made from a length of cloth.

turkey *noun* **turkeys**
A **turkey** is a large bird kept for its meat which is often eaten at Christmas.

turn *noun* **turns**
A **turn** is the time when one person in a group does something.

turn *verb* **turns, turning, turned**
1. To **turn** means to move around.
2. To **turn** means to become or change.

turnip *noun* **turnips**
A **turnip** is a round, white vegetable.

turtle *noun* **turtles**
A **turtle** is a sea creature with a hard shell.

tusk *noun* **tusks**
A **tusk** is a long, pointed tooth like an elephant has.

twice *adverb*
When something is done two times, it is done **twice**.

twig *noun* **twigs**
A **twig** is a small branch of a tree.

twilight *noun*
Twilight is the dim light in the evening before is gets very dark.

twin *noun* **twins**
A **twin** is one of two children born at the same time to the same mother.

twinkle *verb* **twinkles, twinkling, twinkled**
To **twinkle** means to sparkle or shine with a lot of tiny lights.

twist *verb* **twists, twisting, twisted**
1. To **twist** means to turn something round.
2. To **twist** means to bend things around each other.

type *noun* **types**
A **type** is one kind of something.

type *verb* **types, typing, typed**
To **type** means to write with a typewriter.

typewriter *noun* **typewriters**
A **typewriter** is a machine with keys which print letters and numbers when pressed.

typhoon *noun* **typhoons**
A **typhoon** is a very strong, windy storm.

Dictionary fun

Which words start and finish with the same consonant?

?

a b c d e f g h i j k l m n o p q r s t u v w x y z

Uu

ugly *adjective*
Something that is not pretty or pleasant to look at is **ugly**.

umbrella *noun* **umbrellas**
An **umbrella** is a frame covered with cloth which can be folded up or opened and held over the head to keep off the rain.

uncle *noun* **uncles**
An **uncle** is a brother of a mother or father, or the husband of an aunt.

under *preposition*
Something that is below or beneath something is **under** it. *The tunnel goes under the river.*

underground *adjective and adverb*
Something that is below the ground is **underground**.

understand *verb* **understands, understanding, understood**
To **understand** means to know what something means, how it works or what it is.

underwear *noun*
Underwear is clothes worn under other clothes.

unicorn *noun* **unicorns**
A **unicorn** is an imaginary animal that looks like a horse with a long, straight horn.

uniform *noun* **uniforms**
A **uniform** is a special set of clothes worn by all members of a group, such as pupils at a school.

unit *noun* **units**
1. A **unit** is the number one or a single thing.
2. A **unit** is an amount used for measuring or counting. A metre is a unit of length.

universe *noun*
The **universe** is the whole of space and everything in it.

university *noun* **universities**
A **university** is a place where some people go to study after leaving school.

unless *conjunction*
Unless means if not. *I will wear my new winter coat unless it is very warm.*

until *preposition and conjunction*
When something is done up to a particular time, it is done **until** then. *He worked until bedtime.*

upright *adjective*
1. Someone or something that stands straight up is **upright**.
2. Someone who is honest is **upright**.

upset *verb* **upsets, upsetting, upset**
1. To **upset** means to make someone unhappy.
2. To **upset** means to spill or tip something over.

upside down *adjective and adverb*
Something that has turned over so that the top is at the bottom is **upside down**.

upstairs *noun*
An **upstairs** is the part of a house reached by going up the stairs.

urgent *adjective*
Something that needs to be done immediately is **urgent**.

use *verb* **uses, using, used**
To **use** something means to do a job with it.

useful *adjective*
Something that is helpful is **useful**.

usual *adjective*
Something that is normal is **usual**.

usually *adverb*
Something that happens often or most of the time **usually** happens.

Dictionary fun

Which words are compound words (can be split into smaller words)?

? ? ? ?

Vv

vacuum cleaner *noun* **vacuum cleaners**
A **vacuum cleaner** is a machine that sucks up dirt and dust.

valley *noun* **valleys**
A **valley** is a stretch of low land between hills.

vanish *verb* **vanishes, vanishing, vanished**
To **vanish** means to disappear out of sight.

vapour *noun*
Vapour is small drops of water in the air.

vase *noun* **vases**
A **vase** is a container for holding flowers.

vegetable *noun* **vegetables**
Vegetables are plants or parts of plants used as food.

vehicle *noun* **vehicles**
A **vehicle** is a machine for carrying people or things around on land, such as a car or train.

velvet *noun*
Velvet is a kind of fabric that is very soft on one side.

vertical *adjective*
Something that stands or points straight up is **vertical**.

victory *noun* **victories**
A **victory** is the winning of a fight or competition.

video *noun* **videos**
A **video** is a tape that is placed in a video player and produces pictures and sound on a television screen.

village *noun* **villages**
A **village** is a small group of houses and other buildings.

villain *noun* **villains**
A **villain** is a character in a story or play who does bad or wicked things.

vine *noun* **vines**
A **vine** is a long, thin stem that crawls along or around something.

vinegar *noun*
Vinegar is a sour liquid used to flavour food.

violent *adjective*
Someone or something that is very strong and rough is **violent**.

violet *noun* **violets**
A **violet** is a small, purple, yellow or white spring flower.

violet *adjective*
Something that is purple is **violet**.

violin *noun* **violins**
A **violin** is a small musical instrument with strings that is played with a bow.

visitor *noun* **visitors**
A **visitor** is a guest.

vitamin *noun* **vitamins**
A **vitamin** is a substance needed to keep the body healthy. It is found in many foods.

voice *noun* **voices**
A **voice** is the sound made by the mouth when speaking or singing.

volcano *noun* **volcanoes**
A **volcano** is a mountain with an opening at the top from which sometimes come hot lava, ash and gases.

volume *noun* **volumes**
1. A **volume** is the amount of space taken up by something.
2. A **volume** is one of a set of books.
3. The **volume** is how loud the sound is on a radio, for example.

vowel *noun* **vowels**
A **vowel** is one of the letters a, e, i, o or u, or sometimes y.

vulture *noun* **vultures**
A **vulture** is a large bird that eats dead animals.

Dictionary fun

What is the opposite of **horizontal**?

? **?** **?** **?**

Ww

wade *verb* **wades, wading, waded**
To **wade** means to walk through water.

wage *noun* **wages**
A **wage** is the money paid to someone regularly for the job he or she does.

wagon *noun* **wagons**
A **wagon** is a cart with four wheels used to pull heavy loads.

waist *noun* **waists**
A **waist** is the middle part of the body where a belt is worn.

wait *verb* **waits, waiting, waited**
To **wait** means to stay in a place until something happens.

waiter *noun* **waiters**
A **waiter** is a person who brings food to the tables in a restaurant or hotel.

wake *verb* **wakes, waking, woke, waked, woken**
To **wake** means to stop sleeping.

walk *verb* **walks, walking, walked**
To **walk** means to move along on foot without running.

wall *noun* **walls**
A **wall** is solid and upright. It is built to separate one space from another.

wallet *noun* **wallets**
A **wallet** is a small case for holding money and papers that is often kept in a pocket.

walrus *noun* **walruses**
A **walrus** is a large sea animal with two tusks.

wand *noun* **wands**
A **wand** is a thin rod used by magicians.

want *verb* **wants, wanting, wanted**
1. To **want** means to feel the need to have something.
2. To **want** means to need something.

war *noun* **wars**
A **war** is a fight between the armed forces of two or more countries.

warehouse *noun* **warehouses**
A **warehouse** is a large building used for storing things.

warm *adjective*
Someone or something that is fairly hot is **warm**.

warn *verb* **warns, warning, warned**
To **warn** means to tell someone about a danger or problem that is ahead.

wash *verb* **washes, washing, washed**
To **wash** means to make something clean by using water.

washer *noun* **washers**
1. A **washer** is a ring of rubber, plastic or metal.
2. A **washer** is a washing machine.

washing machine *noun* **washing machines**
A **washing machine** is a machine that washes and rinses clothes.

wasp *noun* **wasps**
A **wasp** is a striped insect that flies and can sting.

watch *noun* **watches**
A **watch** is a small clock that is worn on the wrist or carried in a pocket.

watch *verb* **watches, watching, watched**
To **watch** means to look at something.

water *noun*
Water is the clear liquid that falls as rain or flows in rivers to the sea.

Dictionary fun

Which word means something that is below the chest and above the knee?

?

a b c d e f g h i j k l m n o p q r s t u v **w** x y z

waterfall *noun* **waterfalls**
A **waterfall** is a flow of water falling over a cliff or large rock.

watermelon *noun* **watermelons**
A **watermelon** is a large, smooth, green fruit with a pink flesh.

wave *noun* **waves**
A **wave** is a ridge of water that curls over and breaks on the shore.

wave *verb* **waves, waving, waved**
1. To **wave** means to move the hand from side to side.
2. To **wave** means to move up and down or from side to side.

wax *noun*
Wax is a substance that melts easily and is used to make candles and polish.

way *noun* **ways**
1. A **way** is a road or pathway.
2. A **way** is a method of doing something.

weak *adjective*
Someone or something that is not strong is **weak**.

wealth *noun*
Wealth is a lot of money or valuable things.

weapon *noun* **weapons**
A **weapon** is an instrument used to hurt someone in a fight.

wear *verb* **wears, wearing, wore, worn.**
1. To **wear** means to be dressed in something.
2. To **wear** means to damage by frequently rubbing or using something.

weary *adjective*
Someone who is very tired is **weary**.

weather *noun*
Weather describes the outdoor temperatures and conditions like rain, sunshine, wind or ice.

weave *verb* **weaves, weaving, wove, woven**
To **weave** means to make cloth by twisting threads under and over one another.

web *noun* **webs**
A **web** is a net of thin, sticky threads spun by a spider.

wedding *noun* **weddings**
A **wedding** is the ceremony at which a man and woman are married.

weed *noun* **weeds**
A **weed** is a wild plant that grows in a place where it is not wanted.

week *noun* **weeks**
A **week** is the seven days from Sunday to Saturday.

weekend *noun* **weekends**
A **weekend** is Saturday and Sunday.

weigh *verb* **weighs, weighing, weighed**
To **weigh** means to find out how heavy something is using scales.

weight *noun* **weights**
1. An object's **weight** tells how heavy it is.
2. A **weight** is a piece of metal put on the scales when weighing something.

welcome *verb* **welcomes, welcoming, welcomed**
To **welcome** means to show that you are pleased when someone arrives.

well *noun* **wells**
A **well** is a deep hole dug to get water or oil out of the ground.

well *adjective*
Someone who is healthy is **well**.

well *adverb*
Someone who does something in a good way does it **well**.

went *verb*
This is the past tense of the verb 'to go' (see **go**).

were *verb*
Were is a past form of the verb 'to be'.

Dictionary fun
Which word sounds the same as **weak** but has a different meaning and spelling?

? **?** ? ?

west *noun*
West is the direction in which the sun sets.

wet *adjective*
Something that is covered or soaked in water or any liquid is **wet**.

whale *noun* **whales**
A **whale** is a very large sea animal.

what *pronoun and adjective*
1. **What** can be used to ask a question. *What is the time?*
2. **What** can be used to point something out. *Show me what you have written.*

wheat *noun*
Wheat is a crop grown on farms to provide flour.

wheel *noun* **wheels**
A **wheel** is a round object that can turn round and round.

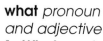

wheel *verb* **wheels, wheeling, wheeled**
To **wheel** means to push along something with wheels.

wheelbarrow *noun* **wheelbarrows**
A **wheelbarrow** is a small cart pushed along on one wheel.

wheelchair *noun* **wheelchairs**
A **wheelchair** is a chair on wheels.

when *adverb* and *conjunction*
1. **When** can be used to ask a question. *When are we going on holiday?*
2. **When** can be used to explain at what time something happened. *She left school when she was 18 years old.*

where *adverb* and *conjunction*
1. **Where** is used to ask a question or give information about place. *Where will the concert be held?*
2. **Where** can be used to give information about place. *I'll meet you where the path enters the forest.*

which *adjective* and *pronoun*
1. **Which** can be used to ask a question. *Which book would you like to read?*

2. **Which** can be used to point something out. *I don't know which shirt to wear.*

whine *noun* **whines**
A **whine** is a long, sad cry.

whip *noun* **whips**
A **whip** is a piece of rope or strip of leather joined to a handle and is used to hit things.

whip *verb* **whips, whipping, whipped**
To **whip** means to beat something.

whirlwind *noun* **whirlwinds**
A **whirlwind** is a strong wind that blows in a circle or spiral.

whisker *noun* **whiskers**
Whiskers are strong hairs that grow on the faces of men and animals.

whisper *verb* **whispers, whispering, whispered**
To **whisper** means to speak very quietly.

whistle *noun* **whistles**
A **whistle** is a small instrument that makes a piercing sound when blown.

whistle *verb* **whistles, whistling, whistled**
To **whistle** means to make a piercing sound by blowing air through the lips.

who *pronoun*
Who means which person. *Who is this? This is the person who won the match.*

whole *noun*
A **whole** is a complete thing.

whole *adjective*
Something that is complete is **whole**.

whom *pronoun*
Whom means which person. *To whom did you give the book?*

whose *adjective*
Whose means belonging to which person or thing.

why *adverb*
Why means for what reason. *Why are you here?*

Dictionary fun

Which words are often used at the beginning of a question?

? **?** ? ?

wicked *adjective*
Someone who is very bad or evil is **wicked**.

wide *adjective*
Something that measures a lot from one side to the other is **wide**.

wide *adverb*
Wide, means fully, such as being wide awake or wide open.

width *noun* **widths**
A **width** is the distance from one side of something to the opposite side.

wife *noun* **wives**
A **wife** is a married woman.

wig *noun* **wigs**
A **wig** is a covering of false hair.

wild *adjective*
1. Things that grow naturally are **wild**.
2. Someone or something that is out of control is **wild**.

wildlife *noun*
Wildlife is all wild animals and plants.

will *noun* **wills**
1. A **will** is a document which states what is to happen to someone's possessions when he or she dies.
2. A **will** is the power or determination to decide what to do and do it.

will *verb*
Will means that something is going to happen in the future. *I will go to the party.*

willing *adjective*
Someone who is ready and pleased to help is **willing**.

willow *noun* **willows**
A **willow** is a kind of tree with thin branches that bend over.

win *verb* **wins, winning, won**
1. To **win** means to come first or beat someone in a game or fight.
2. To **win** means to get a prize.

wind *noun* **winds**
Wind is a movement of air.

wind *verb* **winds, winding, wound**
1. To **wind** means to turn a key or a handle round and round.
2. To **wind** means to twist or bend something around.

windmill *noun* **windmills**
A **windmill** is a mill with large sails turned by the wind to work the machinery.

window *noun* **windows**
A **window** is an opening in a wall, filled with glass.

wink *verb* **winks, winking, winked**
To **wink** means to close and open one eye.

winner *noun* **winners**
A **winner** is someone who wins something.

wipe *verb* **wipes, wiping, wiped**
To **wipe** means to clean or dry something by rubbing it with a cloth.

wire *noun* **wires**
A **wire** is a long, thin thread of metal that bends easily.

wise *adjective*
Someone who knows a lot and can understand things easily is **wise**.

wobble *verb* **wobbles, wobbling, wobbled**
To **wobble** means to shake from side to side.

wolf *noun* **wolves**
A **wolf** is a wild animal like a large dog.

woman *noun* **women**
A **woman** is a female person who is fully grown.

wonder *noun*
Wonder is a feeling of surprise or amazement.

wonder *verb* **wonders, wondering, wondered**
To **wonder** means to think carefully about something.

wonderful *adjective*
Something that is really good is **wonderful**.

Dictionary fun

Which word is the opposite of **lose**?

? **?** ? ?

a b c d e f g h i j k l m n o p q r s t u v W x y z

wood *noun* **woods**

1. A **wood** is a large area covered with trees.
2. **Wood** is the trunk and branches of trees used to make things or to burn.

wooden *adjective*
Something that is made of wood is **wooden**.

woodpecker *noun* **woodpeckers**
A **woodpecker** is a bird that eats insects, which it finds by tapping tree trunks with its beak.

wool *noun* **wool**
Wool is the soft hair on sheep, which is spun into threads and used to weave or knit cloth.

woollen *adjective*
Something that is made of wool is **woollen**.

word *noun* **words**
A **word** is a group of letters or sounds that means something when written or said.

work *noun* **work**
Work is a job that has to be done.

worker *noun* **workers**
A **worker** is someone who works.

world *noun* **worlds**
The **world** is the Earth or a planet like it.

worm *noun* **worms**
A **worm** is a long, thin creature with no legs that lives underground.

worry *verb* **worries, worrying, worried**
1. To **worry** means to be upset or be concerned.
2. To **worry** means to bother or trouble someone.

worse *adjective*
Something that is less good is **worse**.

worship *verb* **worships, worshipping, worshipped**
1. To **worship** means to show love and respect for a god.
2. To **worship** means to love and admire someone.

worst *adjective*
Something that is least good is **worst**.

worth *adjective*
Something that has a certain value is **worth** that amount.

would *verb*
This is the past tense of the verb 'will' (see **will**).

wound *noun* **wounds**
A **wound** is an injury to the body.

wound *verb*
This is the past tense of the verb 'to wind' (see **wind**).

wrap *verb* **wraps, wrapping, wrapped**
To **wrap** means to put a covering of clothes or paper around someone or something.

wreck *noun* **wrecks**
A **wreck** is a very badly damaged or ruined ship, building or vehicle.

wreck *verb* **wrecks, wrecking, wrecked**
To **wreck** means to damage something so badly that it is no longer any use.

wren *noun* **wrens**
A **wren** is a tiny, brown bird.

wrestle *verb* **wrestles, wrestling, wrestled**
To **wrestle** means to fight with someone by trying to throw him or her to the ground.

wriggle *verb* **wriggles, wriggling, wriggled**
To **wriggle** means to move the body by twisting and turning.

wrist *noun* **wrists**
A **wrist** is the part of the body where the arm and hand join.

write *verb* **writes, writing, wrote, written**
To **write** means to put words and letters on paper so they can be read.

writer *noun* **writers**
A **writer** is someone who writes.

writing *noun*
Writing is something that has been written.

wrong *adjective*
Something that is not right is **wrong**.

Dictionary fun
Which word is the opposite of **right**?

?

Xx

x-ray *noun* **x-rays**
An **x-ray** is a photograph that shows the inside of someone or something.

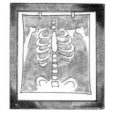

xylophone *noun* **xylophones**
A **xylophone** is a musical instrument made from wooden or metal bars that are hit with hammers.

Yy

yacht *noun* **yachts**
A **yacht** is a boat with sails.

yard *noun* **yards**
1. A **yard** is an area of ground surrounded by walls or buildings.
2. A **yard** is a measure of length equal to 36 inches or 91 centimetres.

yarn *noun* **yarns**
1. **Yarn** is thread.
2. A **yarn** is a story.

yawn *verb* **yawns, yawning, yawned**
To **yawn** means to open the mouth widely when tired or bored.

year *noun* **years**
A **year** is a measure of time equal to 12 months.

yell *verb* **yells, yelling, yelled**
To **yell** means to shout loudly.

yelp *verb* **yelps, yelping, yelped**
To **yelp** means to make a quick, shrill cry.

yes *adverb*
Yes is a word used to show agreement or approval.

yesterday *noun*
Yesterday is the day before today.

yo-yo *noun* **yo-yos**
A **yo-yo** is a toy made from a string wound between two disks. It spins up and down on the string.

yogurt/yoghurt *noun* **yogurts/yoghurts**
Yogurt is a thick liquid food made from milk.

yolk *noun* **yolks**
A **yolk** is the yellow part of an egg.

you *pronoun*
You is the person or people being written about or spoken to.

young *adjective*
Someone or something that is not old is **young**.

your *pronoun*
Something that belongs to you is **your** thing.

yourself *pronoun*
Yourself means you and no one else.

Zz

zebra *noun* **zebras**
A **zebra** is an animal like a horse with black and white stripes.

zero *noun* **zeros**
Zero is nothing and is written **0**.

zig-zag *noun* **zig-zags**
A **zig-zag** is a line that bends sharply up and down.

zip, zipper *noun* **zips, zippers**
A **zip** or **zipper** is a fastening that joins two edges of material together.

zoo *noun* **zoos**
A **zoo** is a place where different wild animals are kept for study and so people can go and look at them.

Dictionary fun

Which word describes two days before tomorrow?

? **?** ? ?

Key Words
Dictionary

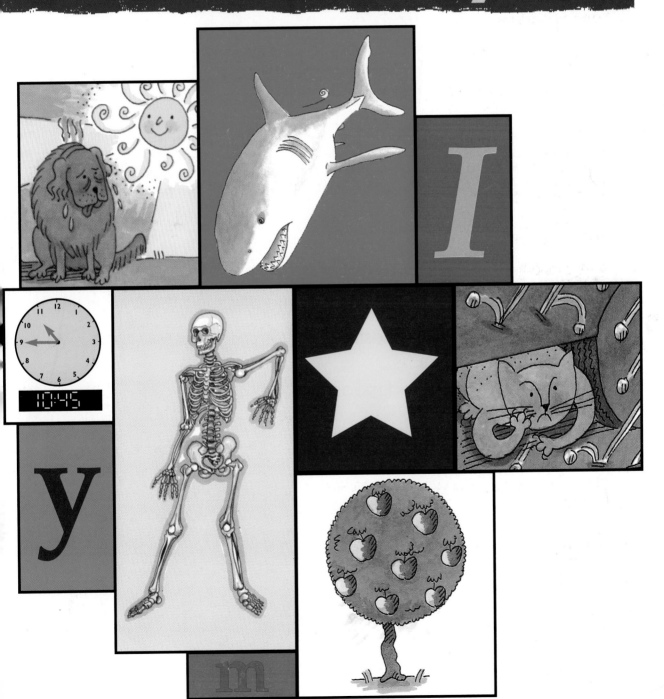

Contents

Dear reader

Use this key words dictionary to help you with your reading and writing. Some of the things you can find more about are listed below.

If you flip the book over, you can use the illustrated dictionary.

The weather

rain

snow

hail

sun

wind

thunder and lightning

fog

cloud

frost

drought

flood

storm

3

The natural world

island

mountain

hill

fields

cliffs

beach

ocean

The human skeleton

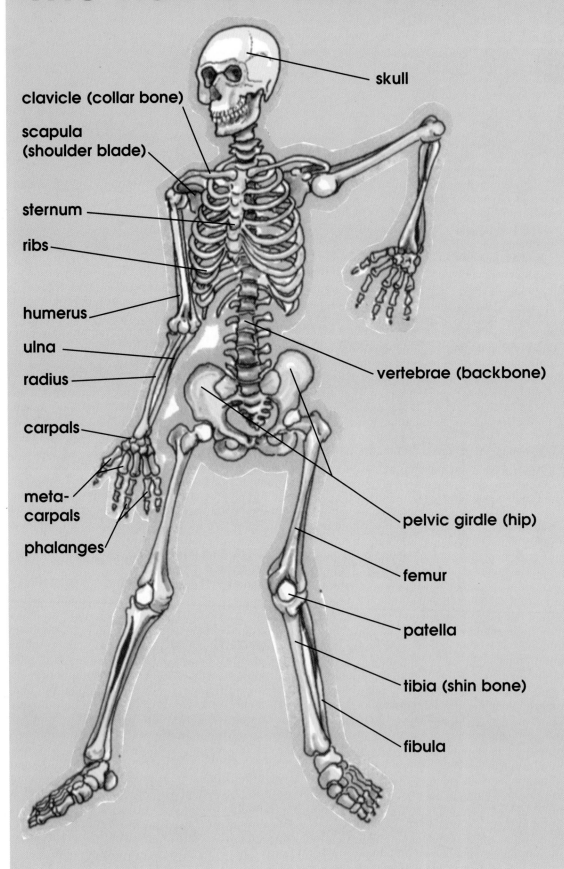

skull

clavicle (collar bone)

scapula
(shoulder blade)

sternum

ribs

humerus

ulna

radius

carpals

meta-
carpals

phalanges

vertebrae (backbone)

pelvic girdle (hip)

femur

patella

tibia (shin bone)

fibula

Inside the human body

The digestive system

Food needs to be broken down before it can be used by the human body. This is the job of the digestive system.

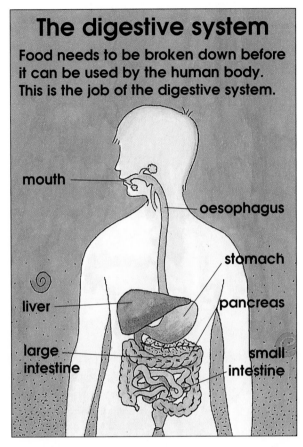

- mouth
- oesophagus
- stomach
- liver
- pancreas
- large intestine
- small intestine

The breathing system

When we breathe our bodies take in oxygen and remove carbon dioxide.

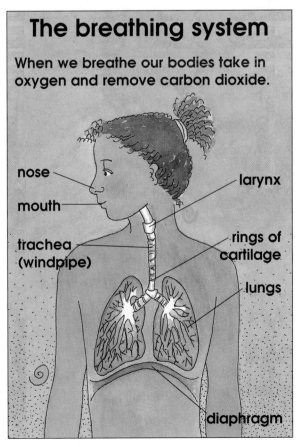

- nose
- mouth
- larynx
- trachea (windpipe)
- rings of cartilage
- lungs
- diaphragm

The circulatory system

Blood is the liquid that carries food, oxygen, waste materials and other substances. The heart pumps the blood around the body through arteries and veins.

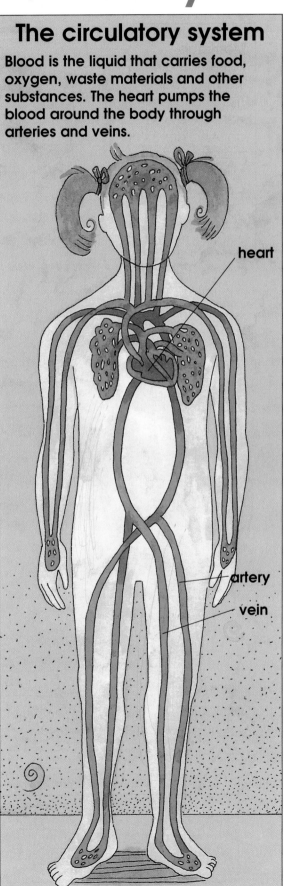

- heart
- artery
- vein

Animal world

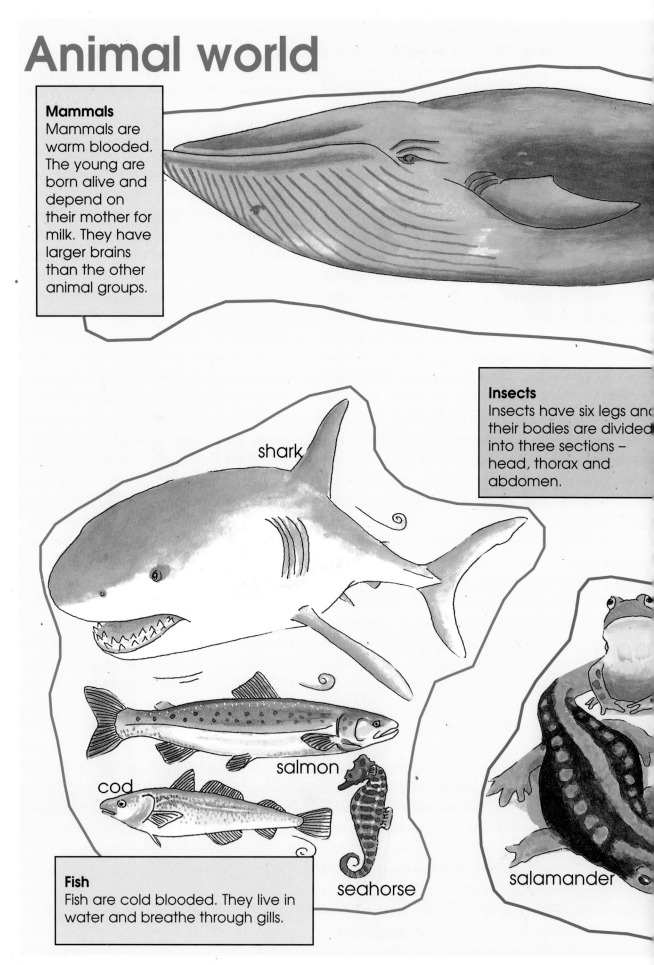

Mammals
Mammals are warm blooded. The young are born alive and depend on their mother for milk. They have larger brains than the other animal groups.

shark

Insects
Insects have six legs and their bodies are divided into three sections – head, thorax and abdomen.

salmon

cod

seahorse

salamander

Fish
Fish are cold blooded. They live in water and breathe through gills.

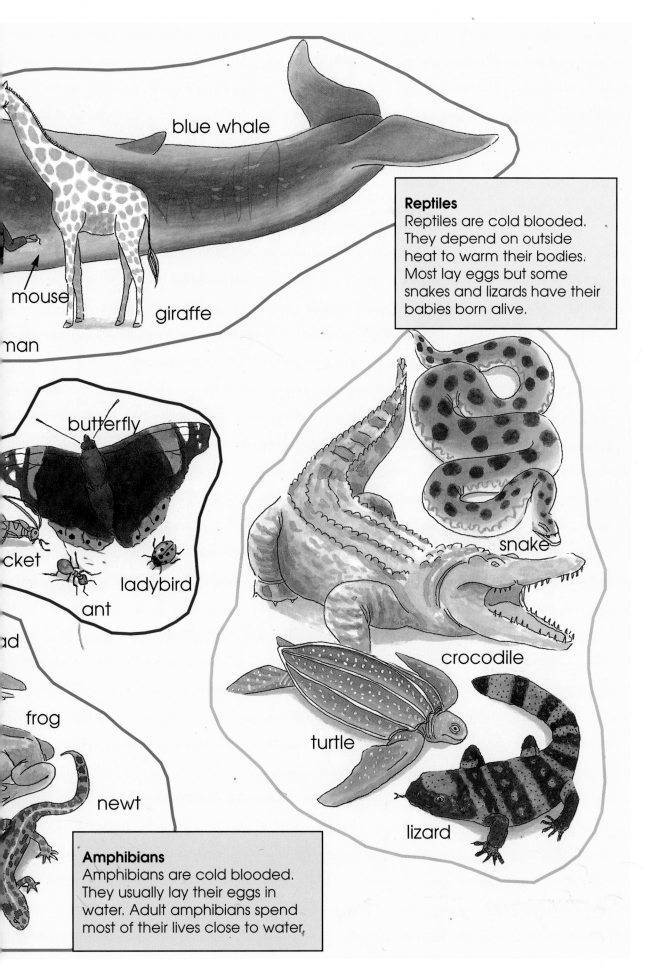

blue whale

mouse

giraffe

man

Reptiles
Reptiles are cold blooded.
They depend on outside
heat to warm their bodies.
Most lay eggs but some
snakes and lizards have their
babies born alive.

butterfly

cket

ladybird

ant

snake

crocodile

ad

frog

turtle

newt

lizard

Amphibians
Amphibians are cold blooded.
They usually lay their eggs in
water. Adult amphibians spend
most of their lives close to water.

Instruments of the orchestra

Shapes and colours

2-D shapes

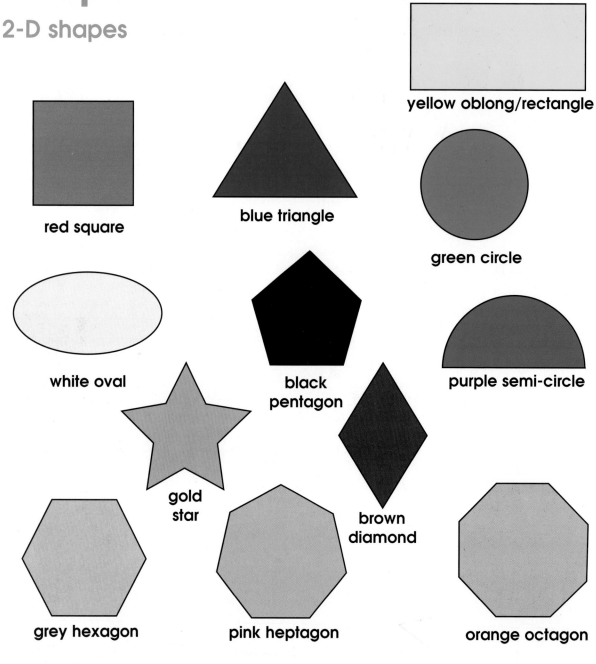

yellow oblong/rectangle

red square

blue triangle

green circle

white oval

black pentagon

purple semi-circle

gold star

brown diamond

grey hexagon

pink heptagon

orange octagon

3-D shapes

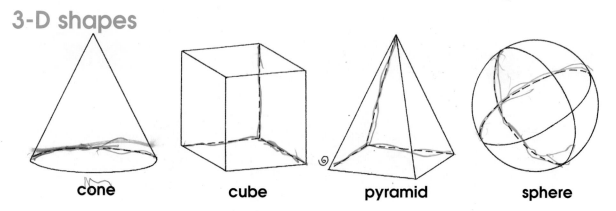

cone

cube

pyramid

sphere

Numbers, weights and measures

Cardinal		Ordinal		Cardinal		Ordinal	
1	one	1st	first	15	fifteen	15th	fifteenth
2	two	2nd	second	16	sixteen	16th	sixteenth
3	three	3rd	third	17	seventeen	17th	seventeenth
4	four	4th	fourth	18	eighteen	18th	eighteenth
5	five	5th	fifth	19	nineteen	19th	nineteenth
6	six	6th	sixth	20	twenty	20th	twentieth
7	seven	7th	seventh	21	twenty-one	21st	twenty-first
8	eight	8th	eighth	30	thirty	30th	thirtieth
9	nine	9th	ninth	40	forty	40th	fortieth
10	ten	10th	tenth	50	fifty	50th	fiftieth
11	eleven	11th	eleventh	60	sixty	60th	sixtieth
12	twelve	12th	twelfth	70	seventy	70th	seventieth
13	thirteen	13th	thirteenth	80	eighty	80th	eightieth
14	fourteen	14th	fourteenth	90	ninety	90th	ninetieth
				100	one hundred	100th	hundredth

101	one hundred and one	101st	hundred and first
1 000	one thousand	1 000th	thousandth
1 000 000	one million	1 000 000th	millionth

Weights

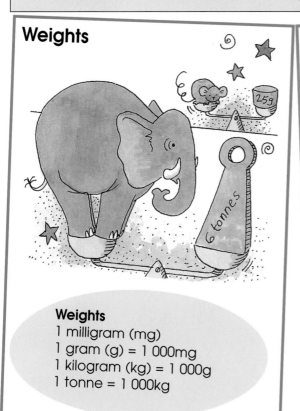

Weights
1 milligram (mg)
1 gram (g) = 1 000mg
1 kilogram (kg) = 1 000g
1 tonne = 1 000kg

Lengths

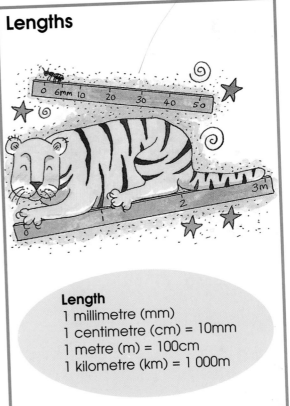

Length
1 millimetre (mm)
1 centimetre (cm) = 10mm
1 metre (m) = 100cm
1 kilometre (km) = 1 000m

Time

Measuring time

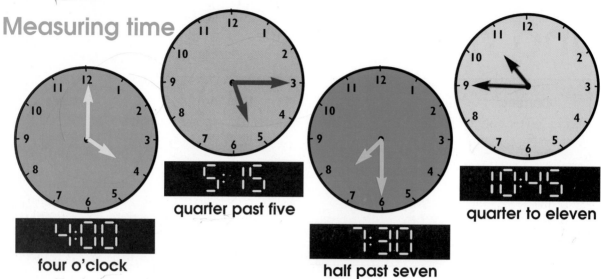

four o'clock

quarter past five

half past seven

quarter to eleven

60 seconds = 1 minute
60 minutes = 1 hour
24 hours = 1 day
7 days = 1 week
365 days = 1 year
366 days = 1 leap year
52 weeks = 1 year
12 months = 1 year

Days of the week
Monday
Tuesday
Wednesday
Thursday
Friday
Saturday
Sunday

Months of the year

January	July
February	August
March	September
April	October
May	November
June	December

Seasons

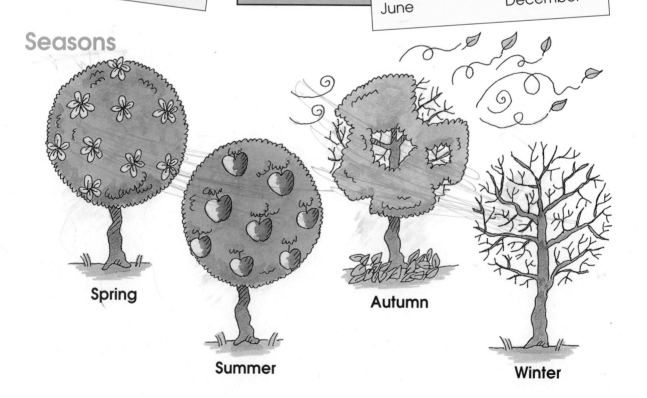

Spring

Summer

Autumn

Winter

The planets

Mercury

Venus

Earth

Mars

Jupiter

Saturn

Uranus

Neptune

Pluto

Mars

Sun

Mercury

Venus

Earth

Jupiter

Saturn

Uranus

Neptune

Pluto

Information and communication technology

speaker

video player

satellite dish

video camera

screen

modem

computer

floppy disks

cd drive

hand scanner

compact disks

keyboard

printer

fax machine

telephone/ answer machine

Contractions

A contraction is a shortened way of writing one or two words.
For example:
  isn't is a shorter way of writing **is not**,
An apostrophe ' is used to show where the missing letters have been taken from.

People use contractions when they speak. If we write the words someone says, we can use contractions. For example:
"Don't eat ice cream before lunch," said Dad.

Some common contractions:

I've	I have
You've	You have
He's	He has
She's	She has
It's	It has
We've	We have
They've	They have

Can't	Can not / Cannot
Isn't	Is not
Shan't	Shall not
Couldn't	Could not
Won't	Will not
Wouldn't	Would not
Shouldn't	Should not
Doesn't	Does not
Mustn't	Must not
Hasn't	Has not
Didn't	Did not
Wasn't	Was not
Aren't	Are not
Hadn't	Had not

I'd	I had
You'd	You had
He'd	He had
She'd	She had
We'd	We had
They'd	They had

That's	That is
Let's	Let us
Don't	Do not
What's	What is

I'm	I am
You're	You are
He's	He is
She's	She is
It's	It is
We're	We are
They're	They are

I'll	I will / I shall
You'll	You will
He'll	He will
She'll	She will
We'll	We will / We shall
They'll	They will

Words we use a lot

Aa

about
above
across
after
again
almost
along
also
always
an
animals
another
any
anyone
around
as
ask
asked

Bb

baby
back
ball
balloon
be
because
bed
been
before
began
being
below
better
between
birthday
both
boy
brother
brought
but
by

Cc

call
called
came
can
can't
change
children
clothes
coming
could

Dd

did
didn't
different
dig
do
does
don't
done
door
down
during

Ee

earth
ever
every
eyes

Ff

fall
father
first
following
found
friend
from

Gg

garden
girl
goes
gone
good
got
great

Hh

had
half
happy
has
have
head
heard
her
high
him
his
home
house
how

Ii

if
I'm
important
inside

Jj

jump
jumped
just

Kk

knew
know

Ll

lady
last
laugh
leave
light
little
live
lived
long
looked
lot
love

Mm

made
make
man
many
may
might
mine
money
more
morning
mother
much
must
myself

Nn

name
near
never
new
next
nice
night
not
now
number

Oo

of
off
often
old
only
opened
once
or

other
our
out
outside
over
own

Pp

paper
people
place
pull
push
put

Rr

ran
right
round

Ss

saw
school
second
seen
should
show
sister
small
so
some
something
sometimes
sound
start
started

still
stopped
suddenly
sure
swimming

Tt

take
taken
than
that
their
them
then
there
these
time
think
those
thought
through
today
together
told
too
took
tree
tries
turn
turned

Uu

under
underneath
until
upon
us
used

Vv

very

Ww

walk
walked
walking
want
watch
water
way
were
what
when
where
while
who
whole
why
will
window
with
without
woke
woken
word
work
world
would
write

Yy

year
yes
young
your
yours